The Fossil Diggings in Swaffham Prior and Swaffham Bulbeck

Bernard O'Connor

Bernard O'Connor

Few visitors to the quiet, rural settlements of Swaffham Prior and Swaffham Bulbeck, or even many of their residents, know of this area's role in the development of an industry of world importance. In the second part of the nineteenth century vast fortunes were made from the digging up, washing, transporting and processing of what were called "coprolites" thought at the time to be fossilised droppings of dinosaurs, fish and lizards! What follows is an examination of the social, religious and economic impact that this unusual industry had on the Swaffhams and surrounding parishes.

Many of Cambridge University Colleges, Cambridge surveyors and solicitors like Charles Bidwell and Clement Francis, local land-owning families and the clergy were very much involved in this unique and fascinating business. What follows is the story of this industry in the Swaffhams.

I have to acknowledge the research work done by David Short of Ashwell Field Studies Centre, Betty Wooton, Richard Grove, Walter Tye, Kathleen Fowle, Albert Sheldrick, Audrey Kiln and B. J. Davey. The Masters, Fellows, Students at Jesus College, Cambridge and St. John's College Cambridge very kindly provided me with access to their archives. I would also like to acknowledge the assistance of the staff at the following institutions: - Cambridgeshire County Record Office, Hertfordshire County Record Office, The Cambridge Collection, Cambridge, Cambridge University Library, Cambridge Folk Museum, Sedgwick Museum, Cambridge, The Public Record Office, Kew, The Valence House Museum, Dagenham, Church Commissioners' Record Office, London, Charity Commissioners' Record Office, London.

Many others in the area have given snippets of information and encouragement but it is to the memory of those who worked in the diggings that this book is dedicated.

www.bernardoconnor.org.uk

Over the winter of 1854 - 5 a new industry started in the fen between Bottisham and Swaffham Prior, small parishes a few miles northeast of Cambridge. It provided a very different occupation to agricultural work, that of coprolite digging and locally called "fossiling." Until the nineteenth century the Swaffhams were small agricultural parishes that had not changed much since the Middle Ages. The spire of St. Paul's church dominated the flat fenland countryside. Over the first half of the century both parishes increased in size. Swaffham Bulbeck's population increased 64% to 888 in 1851. Swaffham Prior, which also included part of Reach at that time, increased 75% over the same period to 1384. Improved health care reduced the death rate and there was a strong tradition of large families in the 19th century. Ten children in the family was not uncommon. There were also strong feelings about social inequality which resulted in a high crime rate and significant out-migration. But beyond the rural communities of Cambridgeshire there were dramatic changes taking place elsewhere .that were soon to affect the Swaffhams.

The 18th and 19th century exodus of the economically active from the countryside to the urban areas resulted in an enormous demand for accommodation and food. The ending of the Napoleonic Wars with the defeat of the French at Waterloo in 1815 brought a period of peace and prosperity to Britain. Its population doubled over the first half of the century. Towns and cities expanded rapidly on the coalfields and alongside the major rivers, canal and railway system. People were attracted by the employment opportunities in industry, retail and commerce following the inventions of the Industrial Revolution. There were also many forced off the land by developments in the Agricultural revolution. The urban population needed feeding. The typical two-up two-down terraced houses didn't have the gardens to grow fruit or vegetables or space to keep a pig or chickens. People needed to buy food from the High Street, the market or the corner shops. Victorian entrepreneurs were quick to recognise the growing demand. Small family businesses dominated the business. As their profits grew they opened more shops, invested in better transport and had more money to buy from the farmers.

If farmers could increase production there was more money to be made. Experiments to increase food production intensified.

One can probably remember from one's schooldays Jethro Tull's seed drill, Lord 'Turnip' Townsend's four-course crop rotation method and the Earl of Leicester and other agriculturalists' crossbreeding that produced enormous pigs, cattle and sheep. But other experiments were going on with plants. The application of science and capital was being expended on agriculture as it had been on manufacturing. Once the chemists acknowledged that phosphate was a major nutrient in plant growth, the search was on to discover new supplies. In 1828 a rock phosphate, called phosphorite, started being exploited in Ontario, Canada. Chemists had found its value as a fertiliser and samples were tested in Great Britain. The German explorer, Humboldt, returned to Europe with details of the South American coastline and his report led to the European's "discovering" the use of "huano" or guano. This was an accumulation of tens of feet of phosphate-rich bird droppings that had impregnated discarded fish carcasses and bird skeletons on the Chincha Islands off the coast of Peru. The locals would not excavate it because of the smell so indentured Chinese labour was brought in. Shipping companies started to import it into Liverpool docks from 1838 where it was sold it at up to £14 per ton. This was much more expensive than bones but a successful advertising campaign in the agricultural press led to its widespread usage.

Other experiments included adding a whole range of materials to the soil. Blood, bones, soot, fish, seaweed, chalk, clay and even rags from discarded wool and cotton clothes were trialled. Maybe one can remember the rag and bone man? It was the waste product of the knife manufacturers in Sheffield, however, that sparked the interest in bones. It was found that the shavings from their knife handles proved a very effective fertiliser when added to the soil. (Voelcker, A. (1862), 'The International Exhibition at Paris,' p.149) The corn mills used by the agricultural suppliers were not able to meet the demand for bone meal and this led to the setting up of bone manure works.

Their most popular products were half-inch bones. These were burnt or crushed and added to the soil as bone meal.

However, the bones from the knacker's yards were insufficient to meet the demand of the nation's manure manufacturers, a factor that led to the import of dried bones. There were reports of cargoes of mummified cats from Egyptian pyramids and sun-bleached bones from the North African desert and the Argentinean Pampas finding their way into the crushing mills. This was enough to prompt the comment by Baron Von Justus Liebig, that

> "Great Britain is like a ghoul, searching the continents for bones to feed its agriculture ... robbing all other countries of the condition of her fertility. Already in her eagerness for bones she has turned up the battlefields of Leipzig, Waterloo, and of the Crimea; already from the catacombs of Sicily she has carried away the skeletons of many successive generations."

(Quoted in Keatley, W. S. (1976), '100 years of Fertiliser Manufacture,' Fertiliser Manufacturers Association)

By 1839 the bone business was worth £150,000 per annum and about 30,000 tons were being imported annually. The Gardeners' Chronicle and Agricultural Gazette gave detailed accounts of the efficacy of these new manures. (Graham, J. (1839), 'A Treatise on the Use and Value of Manure', London p.6) However, tests showed that crushed bones were insoluble. It also took a long time before their mineral potential could be absorbed. Bones were also expensive and the machinery for grinding them had not been perfected. (Ibid.)

Life in the agricultural communities where these new ideas were being practised was not the quiet and peaceful rural idyll that characterised traditional images of country life. There were tremendous economic and social changes brought about in the nineteenth century. The introduction of the Enclosures after 1799 and the implementation of the new technology introduced during the "Agricultural Revolution" had a dramatic impact on rural villages. Many farm labourers became entirely dependent of the farmers for their livelihood. There were "hiring fairs" where men and women were taken on according to the decorations in their lapels. The historian, David Ellison, commented on the "startling" social effects that resulted.

> *"The repeal of the Corn Laws and the lower prices of corn for farmers had made them all try to save costs by mechanisation and reducing their labour forces... Cambridge's farm labourers had often noticed the immense gulf between themselves with their £25 to £30 a year, and the rectors with £300 - £400, comfortable rectories, and often land as well as house servants."*

(Ellison, D. 'Coprolites in the Orwell area,' part of Orwell history topics; Ref. Latter Day Saints Millennial Star, passim, and Kowallis, Gay P. (1970?), 'To the Great Salt Lake from Litlington,' Bassingbourn)

Farm labourers were often provided with a tied cottage from which they could easily be evicted at the whim of the farmer or farm bailiff. Not being seen at church for the Sunday service was a dismissible offence. Going into the public house before the farmer and farm bailiff arrived after church was unwise. Crowds waited at the door in deference. There was considerable poverty and overcrowding in crumbling "shit and stubble" or wattle and daub thatched cottages in many rural villages.

New steam-powered agricultural machinery, designed to save time and labour, was introduced by farmers who were keen to profit from the increased demand for food. These machines like the steam traction engine, threshing machine, deep plough and grain elevator resulted in an increasing number of redundancies in farm labour. Some people developed useful mechanical skills but there was widespread unrest in most rural communities. Many landless peasants were forced off the land when they lost the right to use the open fields. The loss of gleaning rights after harvest, the loss of the common for grazing animals and poultry, the denial of access to the newly fenced or walled in woodland reduced their "free" catch of rabbit, pheasant, partridge, nuts and wild fruit.

The more motivated sections of the community, mainly young adult males and females, left the countryside to find employment in the industrial towns and cities where better paid factory or domestic work was available. Some were attracted by the numerous advertisements in the Cambridge Chronicle and Royston Crow to emigrate. Hard working, temperate labourers and craftsmen were offered employment and land in the colonies in Canada, South Africa, Australia and New Zealand. But it was another enterprise that halted this out-migration and very much brought this area into the Victorian era of industrial and economic change. Most of the villagers were engaged as agricultural labourers on the local farms and large estates or were employed as domestics in some of the country houses of the gentry. Some landowners, like the Hailstone and Haviland families, lived in larger properties with domestics with extensive grounds whilst the majority of the villagers lived in small, cramped, thatched cottages with a small garden for growing fruit and vegetables, keeping a pig and chickens.

When the families got together at Easter and Christmas, for baptisms, marriages and funerals, stories of the changes in rural and urban life would have been common. With improvements in education and increases in the numbers of pamphlets, newspapers and journals there was a growing awareness of the disparity between town and countryside. For those who were unable to leave, some manifested their dissatisfaction with the state of affairs by acts of vandalism. This period, known as "The Swing", after the number of hangings of offenders, saw incidences of farm machinery being destroyed and haystacks, barns and even farmers' houses being set alight. (Fowle, K. (19--), 'Coton through the Ages') However, the discovery of a fossil seam reduced this unrest.

As shall be seen, this dissatisfaction diminished during the coprolite years with higher wages and a variety of new jobs available. What were these coprolites? "Coprolites," as they were called when they were first discovered, were thought to be fossilised droppings. There are numerous variations of their spelling, due in part to the poor literacy of the census enumerator but also to variations in local dialect. They include coprolite, copperlight, copper light, copperlite, coupperlite, copralite, corporolite, coprelite, coperlite, coporlite, coparlite, coprolithe and coperalite. No wonder there was confusion over their origin. (Analysis of the 1861 – 1891 census data) The word came from the Greek "kopros" meaning dung and "lithos" meaning stone. Dung stone - fossilised droppings! Rev. William Buckland, the Dean of Westminster, coined it when he was the first professor of Geology and Mineralogy at the University of Oxford. In 1829 he went on a geological excursion to the Dorset coast at Lyme Regis. Examining the clay and sands exposed by a recent landslip he found the complete fossil remains of an ichthyosaurus. Unusually, it also included its fossilised stomach contents.

Accompanying him on the excursion was the German analytical chemist, Baron Von Justus Liebig. He too was fascinated with the finds but the Dean was obsessed. He had a tabletop inlaid with polished coprolites as well as earrings made from polished slices! It is unknown if he wore them! His dinner parties were very entertaining. A bear used to wander around the dining room behind his guests and a monkey sat on furniture near the window. The menu often included samples from across the food chain, starting from plants and working through the animal kingdom! The worst tasting were reportedly moles and bluebottles! Dinnertime conversations included a challenge to the established religious circles. Buckland had found tiny bones of baby ichthyosaurus in the coprolites. This meant that ichthyosaurus ate ichthyosaurus. They were cannibals! This contradicted the fundamental religious belief that life before Adam was one of peace and harmony. Some argued that Adam and Eve frolicked with dinosaurs in Eden. Maybe the issue was discussed over dinner with Mr and Mrs Mantell who were the first to find Iguanodon remains in Sussex in 1822 and Sir Richard Owen who first came up with the word dinosaur to mean "terrible lizard". Owen was just as eccentric. On New Year's Eve 1853 he invited twenty scientists to a dinner party inside a life-size model of an iguanodon in a London park!

A similar discovery but one with far reaching implications was made in 1842. After Rev. John Henslow, the professor of Botany at St. John's College, Cambridge had been given a living by St. John's in the Suffolk parish of Hitcham, he went on a trip to the Victorian watering hole of Felixstowe. There had recently been a landslip in which he found some interesting fossils in the newly exposed Suffolk Crag at the bottom of the cliffs. There were loads of them. From their smooth, brown, elongated shape he took them to be fossilised dung, similar to those of the ichthyosaurus, discovered by Buckland. (O'Connor, B. (1998), 'Felixstowe's Fossil Industry', Bernard O'Connor, Everton) He suspected that, like animal manure, they would be useful as a manure once they were ground to a powder. He was probably aware from reading about Suffolk's history that the Crag had been used on the fields for generations. In Walter Tye's research into the origins of the coprolite industry he noted that

> "A Suffolk farmer first discovered the fertilizing value of the Suffolk red crag. I prefer that John Kirby, (Suffolk Traveller,1764) of Wickham Market, should tell the story in his own inimitable way :-
>
> "In a Farmers Yard in Levington, clofe on the left as you enter from Levington into the faid Chapel Field of Stratton Hall, was dug the firft Crag of Shell that have been found ufeful for improving the land in this and other Hundreds in the neighbourhood. For though it appears from Books of Agriculture, that the like manure has long been ufeful in the Weft of England, it was not ufed here till this Difcovery was cafually made by one Edmund Edwards, about the year 1718. This man, being covering a Field with Muck out of his yard, and wanting a load of two to finifh it, carried fome of

the Soil that laid near the Muck, tho' it looked to him no better than Sand; but obferving the Crop to be beft where he laid that, he was from thence encouraged to carry more of it the next year; and the sucess he had, encouraged others to do the like." There is no need for me to explain that Edmund Edwards' discovery was soon broadcast throughout south-east Suffolk, where the crag was found. Large quantities were very soon carried and scattered over the heaths and sheep-walks, where the soil had always been hungry and inadequately fed."

(Walter Tye, 'Birth of Fertilizer Industry, 1930, Fisons Journal, p.4.)

Liebig had done some tests on Buckland's coprolites by dissolving them in vitriol, the term then used for sulphuric acid. His analysis of the resultant mass showed them to have a high phosphate content, a mineral much needed in plant growth. John Bennet Lawes, a Hertfordshire landowner, was experimenting with different manures on his estate in Rothamsted. Like Liebig, he too successfully dissolved animal bones, the mineral phosphorite and Felixstowe coprolites in vitriol. The resulting mixture, once dried and bagged, he called "super phosphate of lime". His tests showed that it was soluble in water and that the plant roots could rapidly absorb it. He experiments with it on plants in pots and test beds showed it to be extremely valuable manure, especially for root crops. His "super" was the world's first artificial chemical manure and its application so dramatically increased turnip yields that it became much in demand by the nation's farmers. They were eager to improve supplies of winter fodder. This was because once the harvest was in and farmers knew how much fodder was available over winter, large numbers of surplus cattle, sheep or pigs had to be slaughtered. Meat commanded higher prices over winter until the new stock was brought onto the market in spring. Lawes knew that any way of providing increased fodder would be very popular with farmers.

Much to Lawes' pleasure the results of his tests with his new manure showed that it was effective on a whole range of other crops. He patented his "discovery" in 1842, which annoyed Liebig who claimed to have been the first to do it. It also upset Lawes' mother who was appalled that a gentleman should engage in trade - let alone in manure. Ignoring both he set up his own company. It was called "Lawes Artificial Manure Company." His fiancée could not have been pleased. The planned European Tour for their honeymoon was cancelled in favour of a trip down the Thames during which he spotted an ideal site for his factory. He bought a plot at Deptford and had a large chemical manure works built that was capable of producing up to 200 tons of superphosphate a week. He sold his "super" at up to £7.00 a ton and took legal action against Liebig and others to ensure that anyone who wanted to use his patent had to pay him five shillings (£0.25) for every ton they produced. (Dyke, G.V. (1993), 'John Lawes of Rothamsted' Hoos Press, Harpenden, p.15)

Maybe Henslow was in correspondence with Lawes as he realised that the Felixstowe fossil bed could be a valuable source of manure. As a wide range of animal manure was being put onto the fields he thought that fossilised droppings could be used for the same purpose. In 1845 he read a paper in Cambridge to the British Association for the Advancement of Science. (Henslow, Rev. John, (1845), Report to British Association, Cambridge) It dealt with their potential value to the nation's farmers. Suffolk manure manufacturers like William Colchester, Edward Packard and Joseph Fison took interest. They made arrangements with Felixstowe landowners to have the fossils dug up, washed and transported to their works in Ipswich. A few shillings a ton royalty was offered for the fossils. As a cheap alternative to the other manures on the market, there was keen interest in coprolites.

Maybe it was the reports of Rev. Henslow's speech that prompted a local farmer to show him some fossils that he had dug up on his property. Charles Kingsley, one of Henslow's students, must have been present as he recorded Henslow's response.

> "He saw, being somewhat of, a geologist and chemist, that they were not, as fossils usually are, carbonate of lime, but phosphate of lime - bone earth. He said at once, as by inspiration, "You have found a treasure - not a gold-mine, indeed, but a food-mine. This bone earth, which we are at our wit's end to get for our grain and pulses; which we are importing, as expensive bones, all the way from Buenos Ayres. Only find enough of them, and you will increase immensely the food supply of England and perhaps make her independent of foreign phosphates in case of war."

(Anonymous note in Ipswich Museum's Coprolite file)

A treasure? A food-mine? Such a response must have astounded the farmer. It is undocumented where the farmer was from but it is thought that he was from Burwell, a fenland parish north of Cambridge. Fossils had been found beneath the fenland peat from as early as 1816. (Hailstone, Rev. J. (1816), 'Outlines of the Geology of Cambridgeshire', Phil. Trans. Royal. Soc., pp.243-250) Their discovery was related to an important fenland occupation, locally called "claying". This involved the digging of small pits through the "moor" or "bear's muck", as the bog-earth was called, to reach the clay. This lay between two and ten feet (0.74m. - 3.7m.) below the surface. Wearing waterproofed boots the diggers would use a sharp, cutting-edged shovel to dig through the peat, a light wooden scoop to get rid of drainage water and an axe or "bill" to excavate the clay beneath. The top metre of clay was thrown to the sides of the pit and then mixed into the peat.

The material turned up by this "claying" occasionally included fossils of what were thought to be bears and oxen. When Burwell Fen started to be drained in the early-1800s the excavation of drainage ditches or "lodes" exposed an extensive bed of fossils. A local farmer, John Ball, noticed that the turnips he grew on the clayey, fossil deposit that had been mixed into his peat soil produced dramatically better yields than the crops on fields he had not clayed. The Burwell doctor, Mr Lucas, explained that the "extraordinary liveliness" was related to the high phosphate content of the fossils. ('The Farming of Cambridgeshire,' Royal Agric.Soc.1847, p.71; Lucas, C. (1930), 'The Fenman's World - Memories of a Fenland Physician,' (Norwich), p.25)

Dr. Lucas may well have heard about Rev. Henslow's Cambridge speech or read about it in the local press. Aware of the potential demand by manure manufacturers and maybe even knowing the farmer who had shown Henslow the fossils, he suspected that the Burwell deposit could also be a matter of "commercial proposition". Their shallow depth beneath the fenland peat just above the gault clay would allow them to be raised without very high labour costs. The proximity of Burwell Lode allowed easy access by barge or shallow-draught lighter to Popes Corner - the confluence of the Ouse and the Cam - and then via Ely, Littleport and Downham Market onto King's Lynn and then transhipped to Ipswich, London or elsewhere.

With an eye for speculation and without having first seen it, he bought some eleven acres of Burwell Fen. The locals thought he had taken leave of his senses. A month later, so the story goes, he went by boat up Burwell Lode with "an interested party" to locate the deposit. After rowing for some time, they reached a point about a mile west of the village where the potential buyer was handed a "sprit" and told to push it into the land below the boat. (Gathercole, A. F. (1959), 'Fenland Village,' Fisons Journal, No.64 Sept. pp.24-9; Suffolk County Record Office (SCRO) HC 438.8728/269)

The depth of the seam was not noted but the locals were astounded when he sold the plot and the coprolites beneath it for £1,000. Realising almost £100 per acre was a phenomenal profit, given that agricultural rents ranged at that time from about ten to forty shillings (£0.50 - £2.00) an acre. The "interested party" was William Colchester, one of the Suffolk manure manufacturers who also had investments in brick manufacturing and ships. In 1846 he expanded his manure business by building a new manure works in Ipswich. According to a later geological paper he had raised 500 tons by 1847. (Lucas, C. (1930), op.cit; Reid, C. (1890), 'Nodule Bed,' Memoirs of the Geological Survey (MGS) p.16)

Others speculated in the new industry. Edward Packard, a chemist from Saxmundham in Suffolk successfully processed the Felixstowe "coprolites" and in 1847 he opened his own manure factory on the banks of the River Orwell in Ipswich. Joseph Fison, part of a milling and baking family, had moved into Ipswich in 1840. He established a factory at Stoke Bridge and converted it to process coprolites and other phosphatic material in 1850. (Fisons Journal, No.77, December 1963; Norsk Hydro file, Museum of East Anglian Life, Stowmarket)

Lawes, Colchester, Packard and Fison advertised their superphosphate in the pages of the "Gardeners Chronicle and Agricultural Gazette" and the "Mark Lane Express" thus realising Henslow's idea. Articles on its successful application and of using coprolites in its manufacture appeared in the agricultural press. These increased landowners and agriculturalists' awareness of the financial advantages of locating the fossil deposit on their properties.

So, by the 1850s, Rev. Buckland realised that his discovery had led to the birth of a new industry exploiting fossil beds in Suffolk and Cambridgeshire. He questioned the possibility that these

> *"...excretions of extinct animals contained the mineral ingredients of so much value in animal manure. The question was in fact not yet solved by the chemist, and we took specimens, in order to confirm by chemical analysis the views of the geologist. After Liebig had completed their analysis, he saw that they might be made applicable to practical purposes.*

> *What a curious and interesting subject for contemplation! In the remains of an extinct animal world England is to find the means of increasing her wealth in agricultural produce, as she has already found the great support of her manufacturing industry in fossil fuel - the preserved matter of primeval forests - the remains of a vegetable world! May this expectation be realised! and may her excellent population be thus redeemed from poverty and misery!*
>
> *I well recollect the storm of ridicule raised by these expressions of the German philosopher, and yet truth has triumphed over scepticism, and thousands of tons of similar animal remains are now used in promoting the fertility of our fields. The geological observer, in his search after evidences of ancient life, aided by the chemist, excavated extinct remains which produced new life to future generations."*

(Anonymous author, 'The Study of Abstract Science Essential to the Progress of Industry,' Memoirs of Geological Survey, Mineral Statistics, vol. i, 1850?, pp.40-1)

Many people thought that the fossils were the droppings of bear, lizard or fish or even dinosaur droppings. A retired major from Reach thought that they resembled sun-dried wildebeest droppings. They were similar to those he had seen on the flood plains of the Zambezi once the vast herds had passed. Students and professors at Cambridge University's newly established Geology department became very interested in the range of fossils being thrown up. There was extensive debate in geological circles and many argued that the deposit ought not to be termed coprolite. They should more correctly be termed pseudo-coprolites or phosphatic nodules. However, the trade name "coprolites" stuck. Recently however, an excellent example of some poor creature's rectal content has been found in Barrington that gives credence to the locals' views. One can make out the pressure creases and a sharp point as if it was its last squeeze. Photographs of this and typical Cambridgeshire coprolites can be seen in the illustrations.

The bulk of the deposit was of misshapen, black/grey lumps but amongst them were found the teeth, bones, scales and claws of Jurassic and Cretaceous dinosaurs. They included craterosaurus, dakosaurus, dinotosaurus, megalosaurus, iguanodon and the pterodactyl. Prehistoric marine reptiles of ichthyosaurus, plesiosaurus and pliosaurus were found as well as the remains of whale, shark, turtle and a huge variety of shells, sponges and other marine organisms. The most common was the ammonite. Other animals that were discovered in the diggings included crocodiles, hippopotamus, elephant, rhinoceros, lion, hyena, tapir, bear, horse and oxen - evidence of this area's tropical past. (O'Connor, B. (1998), 'The Dinosaurs on Sandy Heath', Bernard O'Connor, Everton) There were also lumps of what some argue are inorganic calcium phosphate. But why is it that such a variety of creatures that you would normally expect to see in hot tropical countries in Africa were found in Cambridgeshire?

When the European plate broke away from Pangaea about 500 million years ago it was south of the Equator. It was during this period that the gault clay was deposited. This area was about 28° S, where Namibia is today! To reach its present latitude this area has moved over 80° of the planet's surface, thousands of miles. It experienced a range of differing environments on its slow movement north from the tropical and equatorial forests, swamps, savannah grassland and desert to today's temperate latitudes about 55° N. But what had produced such an enormous prehistoric graveyard? A number of the Victorian geologists considered that the Jurassic and Cretaceous fossil deposits had been washed out of the clays which were exposed when the south of England was uplifted from the sea to produce the Weald. A recent theory is that between 96 and 94 million years ago the earth experienced intense, sustained and violent asteroid bombardments. Even 10,000 kilometres away it has been estimated that wind speeds would have been over 100 kilometres an hour for up to 14 hours and temperature increases of over 30 °C would have wiped out anything in the way. Tsunamis, massive tidal waves up to 30 metres high, would have devastated land organisms. (Spedicato, E. (1990), 'Apollo Objects, Atlantis and the Deluge: A Catastrophical Scenario for the End of the Last Glaciation', Quaderni Del Dipartimento di Mathematica, Statistica, Informatica e Applicazioni, Begamo, p.10)

Tectonic changes caused by the impact resulted in sea levels rising dramatically, flooding the London-Brabant Basin, of which present day Cambridgeshire formed its northern coast. This wiped out much of the animal population. Carbon dioxide given off by the flood basalts released by the tectonic activity also played their part. Many of the land creatures would have been poisoned and also the marine life that had to come up to the surface for air. Some suggested that as the bodies accumulated as debris in coastal embayments their bones, teeth, scales and claws gradually absorbed the phosphoric acid from overlying deposits of decaying organisms. Another theory was that the calcium absorbed dissolved phosphate from the seawater. It was said that the rivers had dissolved the apatite, a phosphatic mineral found in the volcanic rocks of Scandinavia and Scotland, which impregnated the deposit and explains their higher phosphate content than today's animal and human bones.

Analysis of amber samples shows that at the time when dinosaurs were at their greatest size, about 230 million years ago, the oxygen content of the air was 35%. Over the Cretaceous period it gradually declined as a result of the increased carbon dioxide released into the atmosphere by extensive volcanic activity. Levels fell to 11% 65 million years ago and today they are 21%. Dinosaurs had to adapt to these changing conditions. It was like having asthma, not getting enough oxygen into the blood. They had to build enough energy to catch prey - the "dash and dine" characteristic of today's crocodiles. Many were exhausted, maybe too tired for sex even. Like crocodiles they buried their eggs. It is thought that increased temperatures meant that they had single-sex populations that further reduced numbers. The leathery skin of their eggs absorbed the poisonous gases and embryos failed to develop. In order to survive these changing conditions dinosaurs had to evolve with a much-reduced size. A cataclysmic catastrophe like a rise in sea level of hundreds of feet as well as poisoned air could explain the huge numbers of creatures found in the East Anglian fossil beds. Given the volume of the creatures, they must have piled up on each other into a layer many tens of feet thick in hollows on the seabed. The upper bodies would have been eaten by any of the surviving marine life like ammonites and worms but the lower bodies, without oxygen for decomposition, gradually fossilised as the upper layers were covered in the hundreds of feet of Cambridgeshire Greensand. This was probably washed into the ocean from the arid parts of the continent still above sea level.

Compressed by this strata and the subsequent chalk marl of Eastern and Southern Cambridgeshire they gradually fossilised. This could explain why there are real coprolites in the deposit. The contents of stomachs, intestines and rectums would have been found along with bones, teeth, claws, scales and shells. Throughout the deposit were found large numbers of ammonites, squid-like creatures that scavenged on the sea floor but there were oyster shells on the upper surface. Over the millions of years, fluctuations in sea level exposed the soft Greensand and differential erosion uncovered the fossils at its base. The remains would have been washed around, so that one does not find whole skeletons in the deposit. Many of the surface features of the remains were removed by abrasion but lines showing worm tracks are often visible along the nodules, the biggest of which rarely extend over six inches (15cms).

Further inundation resulted in a second bed accumulating which was covered once more with Greensand deposits and then hundreds of feet of chalk. This latter deposit was made up from minute marine organisms whose bodies contained calcium carbonate. When sea levels eventually fell these more recent deposits were exposed the to the elements. The upper layers would have been eroded and the chalk and sand gradually lowered to expose the fossil beds. The sixteen ice ages contributed most to the erosion removing hundreds of feet of rock to leave the low chalk and sandy ridges of East Anglia.

Whilst the bed was one of great fascination to the country's geologists, its commercial value was not in how much they could be sold to those Victorians fascinated by fossils. Another of Rev. Henslow's students at Cambridge was Charles Darwin. His evolutionary theories caused a storm when they were published in 1858 and further stimulated the enormous interest in geology, palaeontology, anthropology and archaeology. Many Victorian drawing rooms had specimens from the Greensand displayed in glass-sided cabinets. They were also eagerly bought up by geology students and their professors as well as by museum curators across the country. Perhaps the best specimens can be found in the Sedgwick Earth Sciences Museum in Cambridge.

Their main value, however, was as a raw material for manure manufacturers. And not just in this country but also overseas. In the late-1840s landowners were offered as little as a few shillings a ton for the coprolites. As more and more businesses joined in the rush for manures demand for coprolite rose. Royalties they paid landowners rose to between seven and fifteen shillings a ton in the early 1850s. They depended on a range of factors. The depth, extent, continuity of the seam, the angle of dip, its cleanliness, the nearness to a water source, road, wharf or station, the volume coming onto the market, knowledge or ignorance of current prices and, inevitably, nepotism - how well the contractor knew the landowner.

A new extractive industry began - an alternative and much more profitable line of work than digging clunch, clay or turf. Enid Porter, the local historian, was told that the diggers wore thick union flannel shirts, fustian trousers tied with "lalley gags", a fustian jacket with and inevitable red handkerchief. To keep the rain off their heads and the sun out of their eyes they wore a black cap with a patent leather peak. On their feet they wore fen-type boots with two or three tongues which reached four inches above the ankle. (Porter, E'. Notes in Cambridge Folk Museum on her conversation with C. A. Swann)

When the fossil seam was noticed in the Chesterton brick fields in 1848 the owners sold some of what they considered "troublesome annoyances" to Mr Deck, a chemist of Fitzroy Street, Cambridge for £2 per ton. He probably was not told the royalties the Suffolk manure manufacturers were paying but would have known that similar "phosphatic nodules" were being raised in the Felixstowe and Burwell areas. The tests he did on them showed that the Cambridgeshire "coprolites" had between 50% - 60% calcium phosphate, up to 10% higher than the Suffolk variety. It stimulated their extraction as *"a matter of commercial proposition."* (Cambridge Independent Press (CIP), 18th January, p.3)

When it was found that the seam extended to the south under Coldham's Common in Barnwell, the industry took off on a large scale. Some Suffolk manure manufacturers and entrepreneurial coprolite contractors, keen to capitalise on the demand, moved into the area to win agreements with brickyard and other landowners to raise the fossils. Gangs of experienced diggers from Suffolk came over to run the Cambridgeshire pits. (O'Connor, B. (1998), 'The Dinosaurs on Coldham's Common', Bernard O'Connor, Everton) This in-migration was not evidenced directly in the 1851 census however. There was no reference to fossil or coprolite diggers, coprolite contractors or merchants in any of the parishes where it was then being worked. It is thought that the work was just considered as labouring or, if they were employed by a farmer, as agricultural labour. How many had left the area to find work elsewhere is unknown.

It was hardly a coincidence that the geological mapping of the country started around this time. Whilst the exploration was mainly for scientific reasons, knowledge of the extent and distribution of the Greensand was of commercial importance to those who had money to invest in what was to become known as the coprolite diggings.

The seam averaged about thirty inches (about 39cm.) thick but in places was up to six feet (2.1 metres). In some areas it was non-existent, locally called "dead land," due to a slight rise in the seabed whilst the fossils had tended to accumulate in the hollows. Yields therefore varied. In Cambridge itself it was about 300 tons per acre (0.404ha.). In one pit in Wicken it was 2,000 tons but the average was 250 tons per acre. (Kingston, A. (1889) 'Old and New Industries on the Cam.' Warren Press, Royston p.16) When annual agricultural rents were rarely over fifty shillings (£2.50) an acre and these coprolites could be sold at over £2.00 per ton, potentially several hundred pounds could be realised from an acre! Wages of agricultural labourers at that time wouldn't have been over £25 in a year and £200 could have bought a small estate. No wonder there was a lot of interest in them. So began what has been termed by the historian, Richard Grove, as "The Cambridgeshire Coprolite Mining Rush." (Oleander Press, Cambridge, 1976)

The depth and extent of the bed had to be determined. This was done initially by digging a coffin-like pit. A cheaper method was by using a two-man corkscrew borer. Walter Tye, in his account of the Suffolk industry included an interview with one of the diggers who said that

"To test the depth of the coprolite he made use of a tool like a giant corkscrew, called a 'dipper,' which shuddered in his hands when striking the mineral. Local cottagers always knew what the foreman was after when he came into their gardens carrying his 'dipper.' Naturally, they strongly objected to their gardens being turned topsy-turvy, however much coprolite he might find there, and they were always delighted to see him go. Old residents today say that a sixpenny tip usually had the desired effect."

(Tye, W. op.cit. p.8.)

In places the deposit was found outcropping on the surface but in most cases it had to be dug from between ten and twenty feet (3.7 – 7.4m.) of chalk marl. Where it was found on a small property it was simple matter for the landowner to take on a gang of labourers and have the fossils dug up, washed and sorted and then carted off and sold to a manure manufacturer. In this case it was commonly the farmer's own agricultural labourers. They used to dig the fossils during the low season, once the harvest was in. The work continued over the winter months and then the pits would be left to allow the farm work to start in spring.

If the land was copyhold then the tenant might get permission to raise it using their labourers but occasionally, where a large-scale operation was envisaged, they were evicted and a coprolite manager allowed to move in to the farmhouse. On larger properties an advertisement might be placed in the local press and tenders invited for a contractor to do the work. Occasionally existing tenants were compensated at up to £10 per acre for the loss of revenue from those fields which were being dug. Farmers and others set themselves up as coprolite contractors and took on a gang of men and boys. Pick axes, crowbars, shovels, planks, dog irons (supports for the planks), wheelbarrows, trucks and tramway had to be bought and a horse or steam-operated washmill had to be erected to clean the soil and clay from the fossils. A tool shed was erected and another for sorting, having lunch or sheltering from the rain. All this cost money and local bank managers were keen to make loans to enterprising individuals in an industry that had such high returns.

Women and girls were employed in large numbers where the deposit was found in sandier areas. Here the fossils needed sorting to remove any unwanted stones that would reduce the quality and therefore the price paid by the manure manufacturers. There is no evidence of any female employment in the Swaffhams. The main female employment was in Wicken, a few miles further north on the edge of the fens and in Potton, near Sandy in Bedfordshire.

Contractors agreed to do the work over a set number of years with them paying the landowner a royalty of so much per ton. Once work got started the topsoil and subsoil was barrowed to one side of the field to be replaced later. In many cases it was used as the base of the washmill. As the coprolite seam was exposed the diggers shovelled it into wheelbarrows or emptied it into trucks. These were then pushed by hand or pulled by horses along a tramway that ran out of the pit, along the edge of the field or trackway to the washmill. Here their contents were unloaded to create large piles before they were washed and sorted. The soil above the seam on the new face was removed after undercutting, a process which caused considerable danger. Crowbars, pick-axes and shovels were used to make it collapse and, for convenience, it was just thrown into the trench already worked. As shall be seen there were numerous cases of accidents in the pits caused by collapses. This "backfilling" meant that the labourers gradually progressed across the field and onto adjoining property where a new lease was sought. Sometimes pits were opened at opposite ends of the field and two gangs of diggers gradually dug their way towards each other.

The job of washing the fossils got progressively easier over the years. Initially the technique in Suffolk was to dig a trench into the side of the estuary or the river. The actual washing and screening process was described in Walter Tye's fascinating insights into the diggings.

"That was an old man's job when he became too old for the pit. A long tank some thirty feet in length, was specially provided for the job. The coprolites, along with a certain amount of dirt and bones, were shovelled into sieves which, when full, were placed on a ledge in the tank, just under the surface of the water; to each sieve was fastened a long pole, which the washer pulled backwards and forwards until the stones were clean. When there was a shortage of water, in or

near the pit, the washing was done at the quayside before loading."

(Tye, W. op.cit. pp.3-10)

In Cambridgeshire, without access to a tidal estuary, innovative engineers used their skills to develop sophisticated washmills powered by horse or steam engine. A mound was constructed using the top and subsoil. On top of this mound a circular brick base was laid onto which a circular iron tray was placed. Large sections of the iron plates that formed the base of one such washmill have been found on Rectory Farm, Whaddon. Barrow-loads of fossils were wheeled up the mound and emptied into the tray. A pump was often installed to bring the huge quantities of water needed from a nearby water source. Wells sometimes had to be dug and lined with bricks. At one time there were eleven such mills in operation in the Bassingbourn area which were claimed to have been responsible for lowing the water table of the area. (Whitaker, W. (1921), 'Water Supply of Cambs.' MGS, London, p.84. There is a photograph of a circular coprolite harrow in Cambridgeshire Collection W27.1. KO. 19554)

The working of these mills was described by Mr Lucas, the son of the Burwell doctor, whose coprolite land was the first to be exploited in Cambridgeshire-. Once the coprolite had been brought to the surface: -

> *"The first thing to do was to throw up a hill in the middle of the ground, and this was done by first erecting- a post about ten or twelve feet long, and throwing the soil around it to a height of eleven or twelve feet and of thirty feet in diameter. Three feet from the centre a ring would be formed six to eight feet wide and four feet deep. This would be paved with bricks and the sides would be sheets of iron. On one side of the hill a platform was made from a wooden tank, to which was connected a pump eighteen feet long; a pipe from the tank would go with the ring and opposite the*

tank was a trapped outlet, and on the outer side of the hill a square of about two chains would be earthed up a little to form a sort of pan. From the central post a wooden arm would be attached about twelve to fourteen feet long; to this would be attached a wimpole tree, to which a horse would be yoked. Connected to the centre of the post would be a light rail which was fixed to the horse bridle to keep the horse always in is track; from the arm would be suspended two iron harrows which ran well in on the bottom of the ring.

When the soil containing the fossils was wheeled up to the ring a sufficient quantity of water would be let in. As the horse went round a creamy fluid would be produced and the fossils would drop on the floor. Then the trapped outlet would be opened and the creamlike fluid, called "slurry" would flow into pans. This operation having been repeated a number of times the fossils on the floor would be washed clear of earth and weighed up".

(Lucas, C. (1931), 'The Fenman's World', Norwich, p.31)

The cost of constructing these mills in the late-1840s when they were first developed was £100 but by 1875 the "*coprolite contractors had become so expeditious that a hill could be put up for £5!* (Ibid.) A description of such mills was recorded in a tourist's account of a trip in the fens.

"*As we return from Burwell our eyes rest on several raised circular enclosures, round which a number of often grey horses are almost ceaselessly walking. These are the mills erected for washing the fossils. These fossils or coprolites are valuable on account of the calcic phosphate contained in them.*"

(Eade, D. (18--), 'Rambles in Cambridgeshire', Soham, p.48)

In some areas a less expensive but more efficient process was developed. This was a cylindrical wash mill, rather like an early version of today's vegetable washer. They were in use over in Potton where they were described in an article in the Bedfordshire Times.

> *"... the coprolites are wheeled in barrows to another portion of the ground where a cylindrical sieve is fixed for the purpose of freeing them from the sand. This machine, which is worked by horse power, is a round cylinder of sheet iron, perforated with holes of a quarter inch diameter and placed horizontally in a tank of water, the cylinder being half submerged. The drum of the cylinder is two ft. in diameter at the larger end and 1 ft. at the smaller and 10 ft. in length.*
>
> *The fossils are put in at the larger end, and as the drum revolves the smallest stones and the sand fall through the holes into the water tank, and the larger are carried along by a screw arrangement, and emptied at the smaller end into barrows. When these are filled they are wheeled by men into the sorting sheds where women are engaged in sorting. These sheds, 28 ft. long by 8 ft. wide, have on each side a bench, separated by partitions with room for one woman to work.*
>
> *The fossils being largely mixed with sandstones, it is necessary that they should be removed before they are ready for market. The fossils in their mixed state, are emptied on the benches and sorted, the stones being thrown onto the floor and the fossils passed through a hole at the back of the benches into a box outside. They are then wheeled into heaps ready for sale.*

(Bedfordshire Times, May 18th 1962. from an original article in 1878)

As the technology improved, those contractors who could afford it, used steam powered washmills. After several such washings the dirty water, locally termed "slub" or "slurry" was run back into "slurry pans" to dry out before the topsoil was replaced. The theory was that once dried the cracks in it would allow better drainage. As the work progressed across the field the mill was transferred to a more accessible site. The topsoil was barrowed back into the trench or slurry pit and levelled ready for cultivation. Whilst the theory was that this process would improve the soil, in practise the operation was not always done thoroughly. It was cheaper for a contractor to cover it up quickly and move on. A farmer, however, would take care as he would benefit from improved cropping. In several areas white chalk markings can still be seen on the fields which indicate where slurry was not properly covered or the topsoil replaced. Astute land agents ensured that agreements included very precise instructions for this process and subsequent drainage, levelling and seeding.

As the first bridge across the river between Cambridge and Ely was not built until 1871 and the railway did not reach this area east of the River Cam until 1884 horses were a common sight hauling tumbrils loaded with washed coprolites along the lode side tracks to the nearest wharf. The network of drains and navigable lodes made transport in this area considerably easier than on other parts of the coprolite belt. Access by the lodes to the Cam and Ouse was of great advantage. At the wharves they were either emptied directly into the holds of barges or lighters or shovelled into barrows and then wheeled up planks and emptied into them. As mentioned earlier this new traffic proved a welcome boost to the owners of barges and fenland lighters. In an account of the Fens it was stated that "*In the latter part of the nineteenth century a decline in river trade was temporarily arrested by the shipping of coprolites.*" (R.C.H.M., 'County of Cambs.', p.109a.) If contractors wanted them sent by rail then they had to get them across the ferry at Clayhithe and then over to Waterbeach Station.

Some were taken south to manure factories in Cambridge but most went north via King's Lynn to Ipswich, London and elsewhere. Some may have been carted direct to local bone mills like Walton's on East Road in Cambridge or the Cambridge Manure Company's works on Histon Road. John Rolfe Mann, the Cambridge auctioneer, A. P. Chaplin, a Fulbourn merchant and other "agriculturalists" and entrepreneurs who recognised the profits to be made in this lucrative business, set up this company in the early-1850s. The Cambridge solicitor, Clement Francis, agreed to act as their "undisclosed agent." (Cambridge Collection, Cooper's Misc. Papers, 32. 1856; Cambridgeshire County Record Office (CCRO), Francis & Co. Bill Books, 1855 pp.455,539; CCRO R60/3 Cambridge Manure Co. Minute Books.) Many local bone and corn mills had to be converted as the gritstone was not hard enough to grind the coprolites. A hard buhrstone had to be installed in its place.

With "super" being sold at up to £7 a ton, half the price of guano, it became much in demand across the country. It was not long therefore before sales were being promoted across Europe, in America and throughout the Empire. There were reports of sales as far afield as Russia and Queensland. (O'Connor, B. (1998) 'The Dinosaurs on Coldham's Common', Bernard O'Connor, Everton) During the 1850s there were four manure factories in Cambridge. With them paying an average forty-three shillings and sixpence (£2.18) a ton in 1856 for Cambridge coprolites there were profits to be made by coprolite contractors and merchants. By the 1870s the Greensand deposit had been mapped in most of the Eastern Counties. Although the Upper and Lower Greensand beds were not continuous, the fossils at their base were worked in parts of Suffolk, Norfolk, Cambridgeshire, Hertfordshire, Bedfordshire, Buckinghamshire, Oxfordshire, Hampshire, Yorkshire and Kent. Its enormous extent allowed many new manure companies to capitalise on this new raw material and take a share of the increasing market for artificial fertilisers. Accordingly, many new chemical manure works were opened on the coprolite belt in Burwell, Duxford, Shepreth, Royston, Bassingbourn and Odsey. The extent of the coprolite belt across this area can be seen in the illustrations.

One of Cambridge's iron founders, James Ind Headly, who built the famous Eagle steam engine, was very much involved in the coprolite business. He had his own coprolite works erected behind his Eagle Foundry on Mill Road in Cambridge and had his works, "*well fitted up to make the pumps, washmills, cast iron*

Lower Cretaceous Terrestrial Communities
a *Iguanadon* (Vertebrata: Reptilia: Archosaur – dinosaur)
b *Megalosaurus* (Vertebrata: Reptilia: Archosaur – dinosaur)
c *Hypsilophodon* (Vertebrata: Reptilia: Archosaur – dinosaur)
d *Acanthopholis* (Vertebrata: Reptilia: Archosaur – dinosaur)
e *Equisetites* (Pteridophyta: Calamites – horsetails)

(McKerrow, W.S.. (1978), *The Ecology of Fossils: An Illustrated Guide*, Duckworth, p.297)

The Fossil Diggings in Swaffham Prior and Swaffham Bulbeck

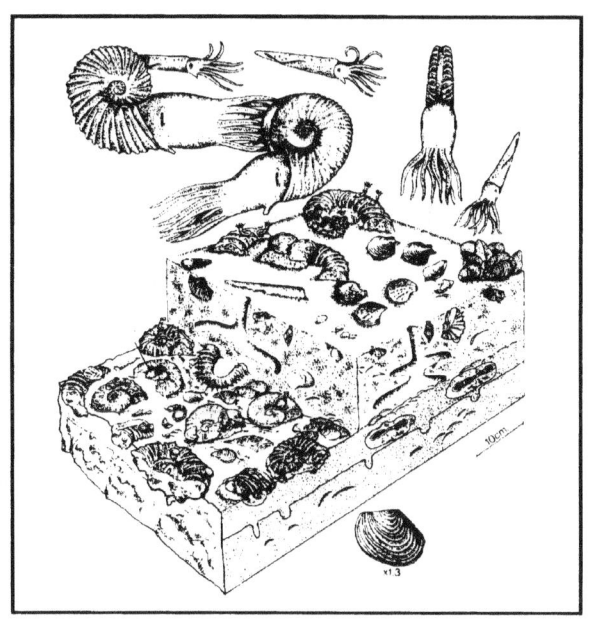

The Phosphate bed Community
(McKerrow, W.S.. (1978), *The Ecology of Fossils: An Illustrated Guide*, Duckworth, p.286)

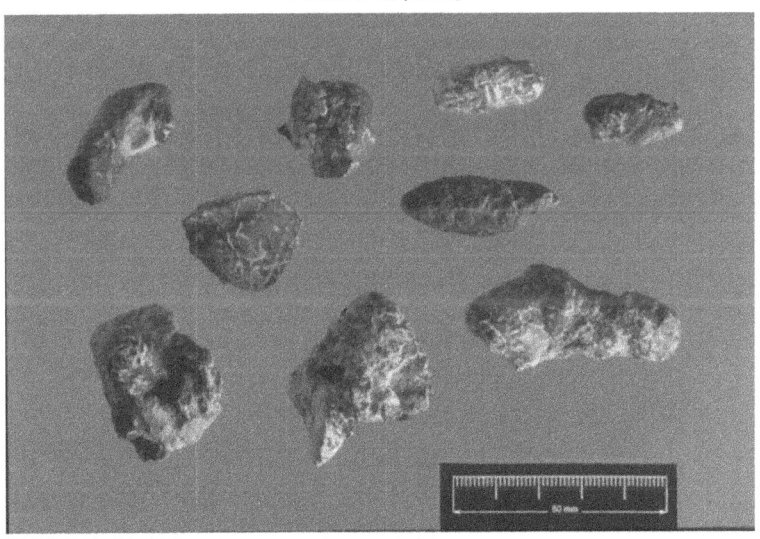

Cambridgeshire coprolites. (Photograph courtesy of Earth Sciences Museum, Cambridge)

Cambridgeshire coprolites, thought to be 170 million years old. (Courtesy of Tim Gane)

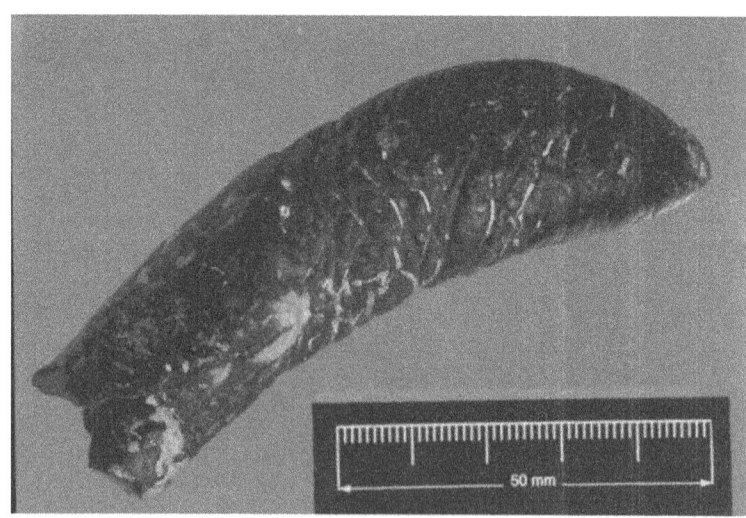

The Barrington coprolite
(Photograph courtesy of Earth Sciences Museum, Cambridge)

The Fossil Diggings in Swaffham Prior and Swaffham Bulbeck

Coprolite Diggings at Orwell, Cambridgeshire. 1860s – 1870s
(Courtesy of Cambridgeshire Collection W27.1J80 25358)

Coprolite Diggings in Cow Pasture, Abington Pigotts, Cambridgeshire, 1883
(Courtesy of Mr and Mrs Sclater, Abington Pigotts)

Photographs of the coprolite works on Sandy Heath, Bedfordshire, c.1882) The top photo shows women outside the sorting shed. The lower photographs shows a horse-powered cylindrical washmill. (Courtesy of Potton History Society)

Undated photograph of windmills in Bassingbourn, which, once the harvest had been milled, the millstones were replaced with buhr-stones to grind the coprolites. Horse-drawn carts brought the coprolites along the road from diggings in nearby parishes.

Undated postcard of Bird's manure factory at Duxford, which was used to grind local coprolites and produce superphosphate.

Steam engine hauling coprolites from Whaddon to Shepreth Station c.1880 (Cambridge Collection Q AR J8 11029 Courtesy of Mrs Coningsby, Whaddon

Undated postcard of horse-drawn tumbrils carrying coprolites to the railway station at Millbrook, Bedfordshire.

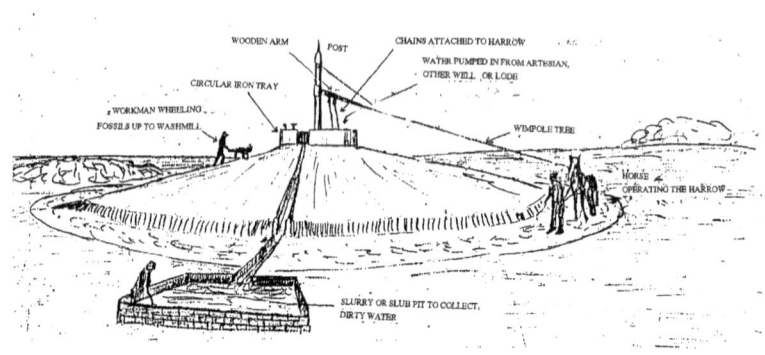

(Based on sketch in Richard Grove's Cambridgeshire Coprolite Mining Rush)

Undated photograph of a circular coprolite harrow
Cambridgeshire Collection: W27.1. KO. 19554).

The Fossil Diggings in Swaffham Prior and Swaffham Bulbeck

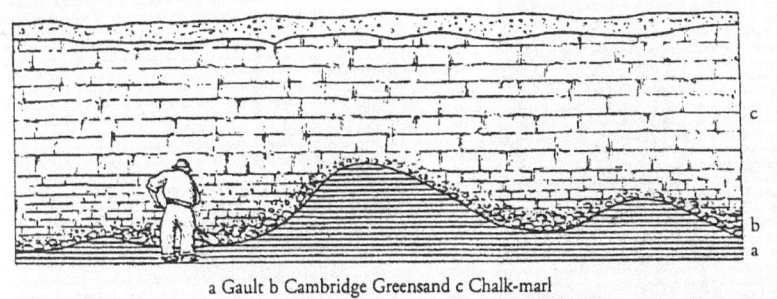

a Gault b Cambridge Greensand c Chalk-marl

View of a coprolite pit in Horningsea, Cambs.
(Jukes-Browne, A.J. & Hill, W. *Cretaceous Rocks of Britain,* Mem. Geol. Surv. 1903, p.194)

Undated photograph of coprolite diggers in Orwell, Cambridgeshire
(Courtesy of Sue Miller, Orwell History Society)

Photographs of the coprolite works on Sandy Heath, Bedfordshire, c.1882) The top photo shows women outside the sorting shed. The lower photographs shows a horse-powered cylindrical washmill. (Courtesy of Potton History Society)

Caricature of J.B. Lawes who patented the technique of dissolving coprolite and other phosphatic materials in sulphuric acid to produce superphosphate. He set up his own manure company, won contracts to raise coprolites and purchased others from diggings across south-east England (*Vanity Fair* 8th July 1882)

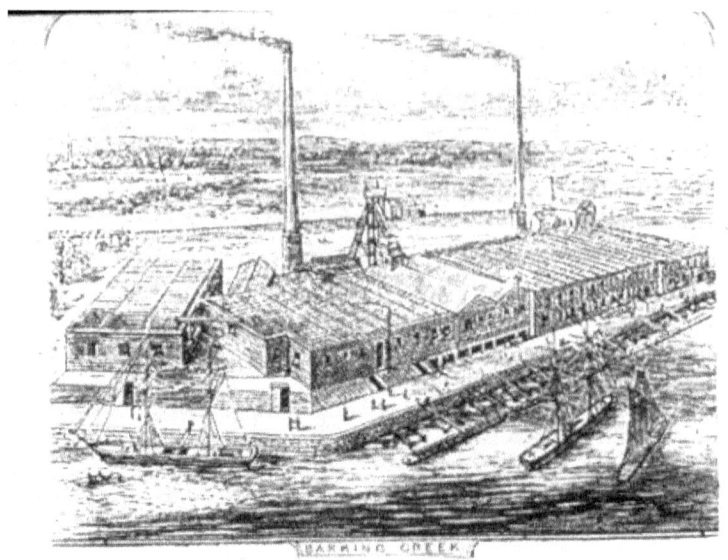

LAWES' MANURE FACTORY, DEPTFORD CREEK.

(Courtesy of Lawes Agricultural Trust, Rothamsted Agricultural Station)

Undated photograph of coprolites being unloaded at Lawes'
Chemical Manure Works at Barking, London
(Courtesy of Rural History Centre, Reading University Neg. No. 35/23594)

R. & H. WALTON,
MANUFACTURERS OF ALL KINDS OF
MANURES,
EAST ROAD, AND COLDHAM ROAD, CAMBRIDGE.

Blood Manure, Corn Manure, Turnip Manure, Mangold Manure,
SUPERPHOSPHATE OF LIME,
PREPARED NIGHT SOIL FOR CORN.

The following articles supplied in any quantity for mixing purposes:—
Half Inch Bones; Quarter Inch Bones; Sulphuric Acid; Muriatic Acid; Sulphate of Ammonia; Agricultural Salt; Soot; &c., &c.

Experienced Men sent out for mixing if required.
BONE AND MANURE WORKS,
EAST ROAD, AND COLDHAM ROAD, CAMBRIDGE.

Robert Walton's advert, Kelly's Post Office Directory 1864

Undated photograph of Edward Packard (1819 – 1899) who founded Edward Packard and Company. In 1843 he began making superphosphate by dissolving old bones in sulphuric acid at Snape Mill. In 1851 he built Britain's first complete sulphuric acid and superphosphate works at Bramford and went on to win coprolite agreements and purchase coprolites from across southeast England.
(http://www.yara.com/en/about/yara_centennial/heritage/fisons_inter.html)

1861 photograph of William Colchester (1813–1898), one of the first manure manufacturers to use Suffolk coprolites. Had manure works in Ipswich, moved into Cambridgeshire fens in 1846, won coprolite contracts and purchased others from diggings across southeast England.
(Courtesy of Giles Colchester)

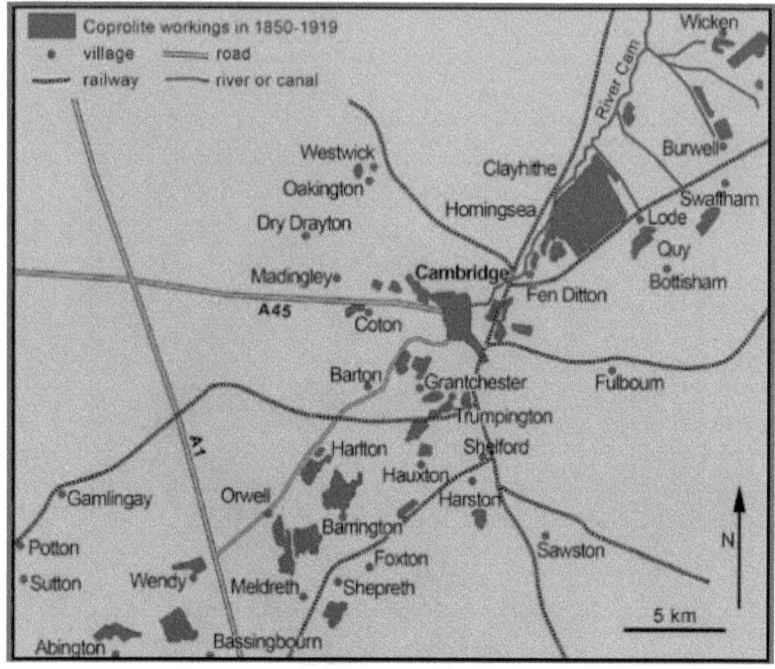

The extent of the coprolite diggings across Cambridgeshire
(Grove, R. (1976), The Cambridgeshire Coprolite Mining Rush,
Oleander Press)

Extract from geological map of south-west Cambridgeshire after Woodward (1904 based on Reynolds (Ian West 2001)
6 = Chalk; 7 = Upper Greensand; 8 = Lower Greensand

PARTICULARS

OF

HIGHLY DESIRABLE INVESTMENTS

CONSISTING OF

Several Allotments and Inclosures of Remarkably Productive

ACCOMMODATION LAND

WITH VALUABLE BEDS OF

COPROLITE & CLUNCH

Comprising an Area of about FIFTY ACRES of

ARABLE AND GRASS LAND

ALL

TITHE-FREE & principally FREEHOLD

ELIGIBLY SITUATE IN THE PARISHES OF

SWAFFHAM PRIOR & BOTTISHAM

IN THE COUNTY OF CAMBRIDGE.

To be Sold by Auction, by

MR. J. CARTER JONAS

On FRIDAY, the 1st day of July, 1859,

AT THE RED LION INN, SWAFFHAM PRIOR,

At SIX for SEVEN o'clock punctually, in NINE LOTS.

By direction of the Trustees and Executors of the Will of Mr. Stephen Danby, deceased.

Particulars and Conditions of Sale may be obtained of CLEMENT FRANCIS, Esq., Solicitor, Emmanuel Street, Cambridge, and of Mr. J. CARTER JONAS, Land Agent, &c., Cambridge and Newmarket.

PRINTED BY JONATHAN PALMER, SIDNEY STREET, CAMBRIDGE.

CCRo. R51.25.31(6)

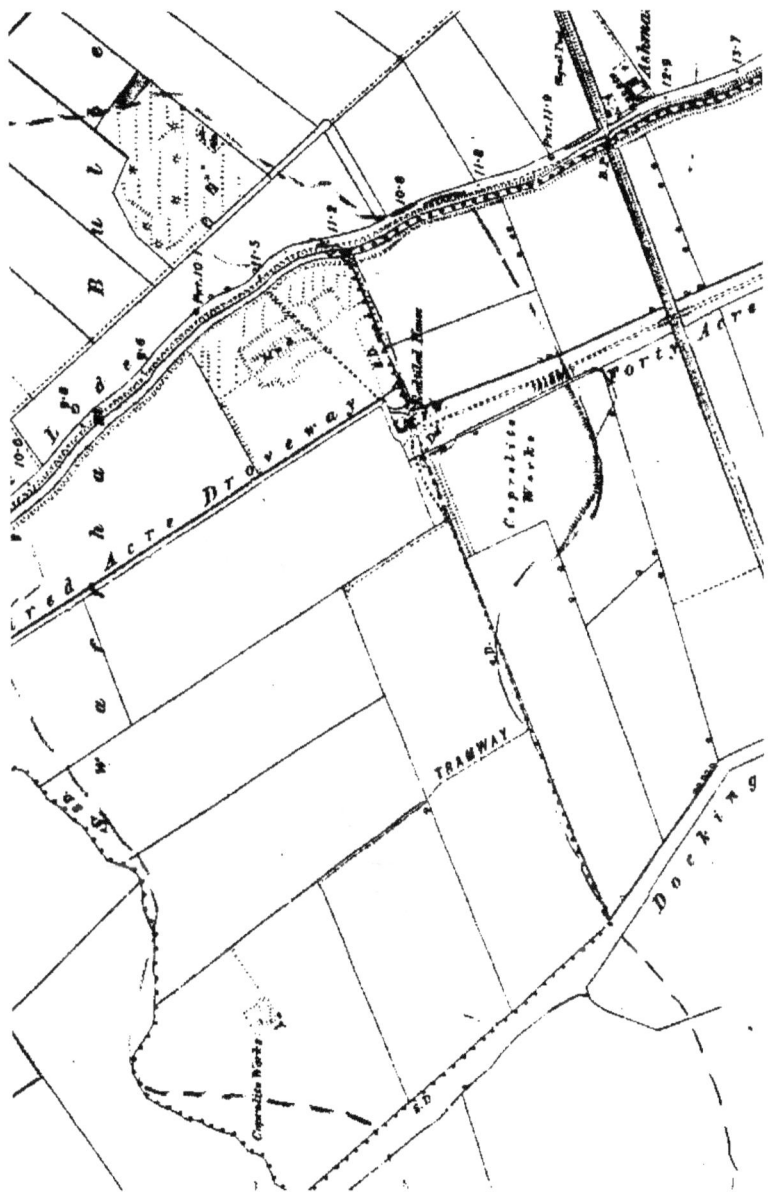

Two coprolite works and tramway marked on 1st edition 6-inch map of Cambs.

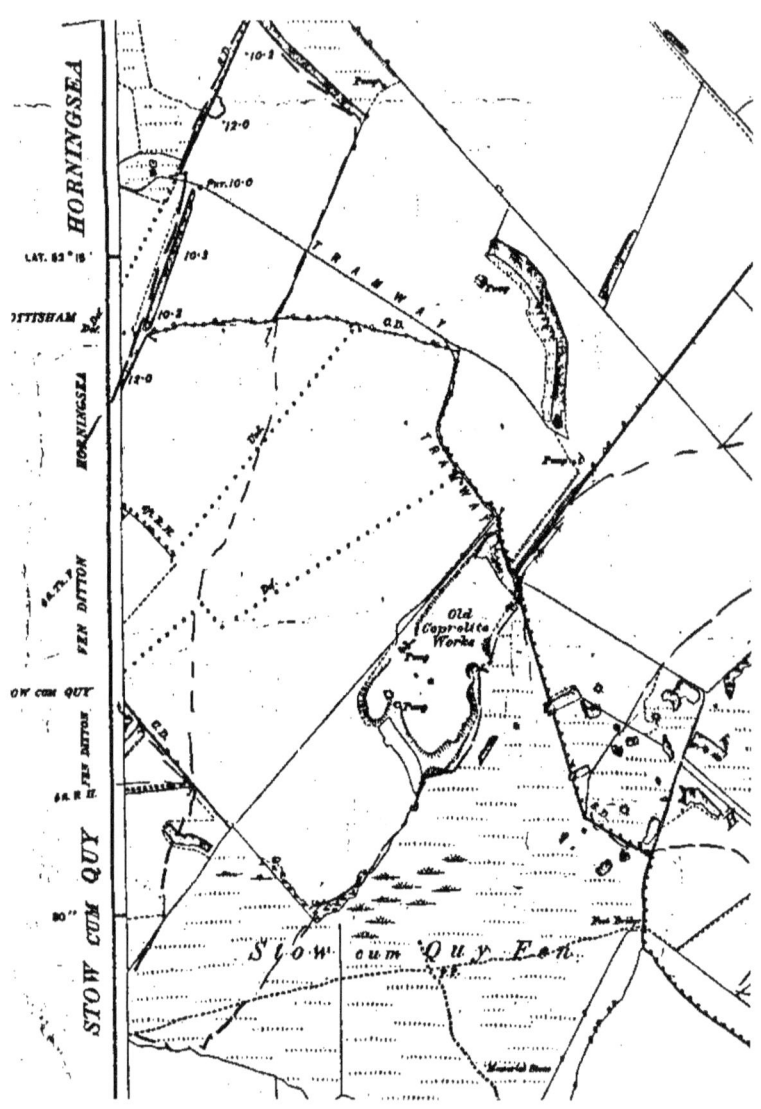

Extract from 1st Edition OS map showing Quy Fen coprolite works, water-filled trenches, old washmill sites and the tramway to the River Cam at Clayhythe

QUY FEN COPROLITE WORKS.

Rules to be observed by the workers and to be signed by each one on his entering upon his engagement with the Committee named in the Licence from Mrs. Francis.

1. Each worker shall be engaged from week to week—the week commencing on Monday morning. Any worker who may be taken on in the middle of the week shall recommence his engagement as from the following Monday morning.

2. The workers shall be engaged on behalf of the Committee by their foreman or manager for the time being.

3. Each worker shall work diligently, and under the directions and to the satisfaction of the foreman.

4. Except on Saturdays the working hours shall be from 6.30 a.m. to 4.30 p.m., from the 1st of March to the end of September, and from 7 a.m. to 4.30 p.m. from the 1st of October to the end of February. On Saturdays the work shall commence at 6.30 a.m. or 7 a.m., according to the time of year, but shall always close at 1 p.m.

5. The work is to be paid for by the yard, pitmen to receive $2\frac{3}{4}d$. per yard, and second soilers $3d$. per yard.

6. The pitmen shall carry their work down 4 feet wide, and shall not throw stones before or after the regular working hours, unless expressly authorised by the foreman so to do. Any pitman transgressing this rule shall forfeit his hag.

7. The second soilers shall keep their work well back. Any second soiler transgressing this rule shall for the first offence forfeit his hag, and for the second offence shall be liable to be reported to the Committee.

8. No worker shall enter the engine shed, unless expressly authorised by the foreman, or unless he have some special business.

9. The foreman is authorised by the Committee summarily to dismiss any worker introducing dog or gun upon the works, or found in pursuit of game upon the land in the neighbourhood of the works.

10. The foreman is authorised also to dismiss summarily any worker who shall maliciously damage barrows or other plant, and such worker shall be liable to prosecution by the Committee.

11. The foreman is authorised to suspend for any period not exceeding one week any worker who shall neglect his work, or who shall disobey these rules or the directions of the foreman, or who shall be drunk upon the works, or who shall be quarrelsome or riotous, or who shall use oaths or bad language to the annoyance of others, or who shall illtreat a horse, or who shall otherwise misconduct himself. Any worker who shall be suspended by the foreman, shall be liable to be reported to the Committee and, if suspended for the second time, shall in any case be reported to the Committee.

12. Any worker who shall be reported to the Committee shall be liable to instant dismissal, and shall be entitled only to the wages which he shall have earned up to the time of his suspension by the foreman.

I hereby engage with the Committee upon these terms and I undertake to observe the rules above set forth.

(CCRO. R89/40)

(Courtesy of Cambs.R.O.)

POOR'S FEN, QUY, CAMBS.

CATALOGUE OF ALL THE VALUABLE

COPROLITE PLANT

COMPRISING

About 20 tons of Tramway Rails, 40 Barrows, 10 Trucks, 70 Planks, 60 long Slurry Troughs, 40 Hoisting Frames, 25 Crow-bars, 10 large Tubs, and Tanks, Washing Mill and Slurry Wheel, complete,

2 WELL-BUILT ENGINE HOUSES,
2 TIMBER-BUILT STABLES,
LARGE MESS ROOM,
AND

5 in. and 7 in. Centrifugal Pumps,

CAPITAL 10-H.P. PORTABLE ENGINE,

Quantity of Cast-Iron Piping, 6 Driving Straps, and numerous other Effects.

WHICH MESSRS.

WRIGHT AND SCRUBY

Are instructed to sell by Auction, upon the Works, close to Quy Station, G.E.R.

ON TUESDAY, OCTOBER 30th, 1894,

At Eleven o'clock in the Morning.

Catalogues may be obtained of the AUCTIONEERS, Cambridge and March.

J. Webb & Co., Printers, Alexandra Street, Cambridge.

(Cambridge Weekly, 12th October, 1894)

The Fossil Diggings in Swaffham Prior and Swaffham Bulbeck

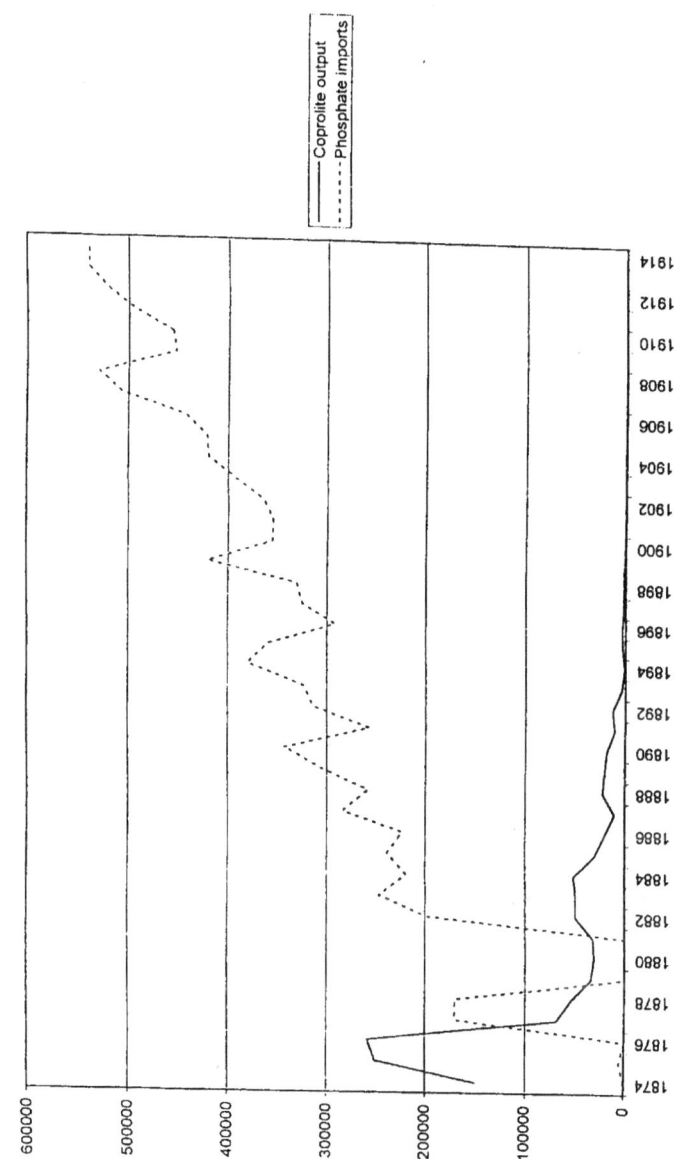

Coprolite Production and Phosphate Imports 1874-1914

screens and steam engines to provide power." (Enid Porter's notebooks Cambridge Folk Museum 15/64-65) To capitalise on the demand William Colchester expanded his business interests to include a chemical manure works in Burwell and an iron foundry in Bassingbourn. The latter provided much of the plant and machinery needed in the works. Headly was aware of the investment opportunities in this area and luck had it that one of his relatives lived in Coton whose land was dug for coprolites. In the early-1850s coprolite contractors were paying landowners royalties of between seven and fifteen shillings a ton for all the coprolites they raised. This entailed having a weighbridge set up by the works and for accurate measurements to be recorded. To avoid errors and dependence on the contractors' weighings the land agents suggested an alternative scheme whereby royalties should be paid according to how many acres were dug over the year. This entailed having the pits surveyed around Lady Day (May 1st) and Michaelmas (September 29th). The surveyor's measurements could then be used to determine how much the contractor owed. This provided local companies like Bidwell, Francis, Smith, Carter Jonas and Mann and Raven a valuable additional source of income for the next forty years. Royalties ranged from as high as £400 to as low as £30 an acre but the average was about £100. This was about forty to fifty times the revenue the landowners could get from agricultural rents. After labour and other costs were deducted the contractors could make a big profit.

Throughout the 1850s the seam was worked in Cambridge and some nearby parishes. With the development of mass-production in the brick and tile making industry, landowners were able to bring a lot more clay land under cultivation. Laying down drainage tiles did this. The trenching work for this, or deep ploughing, often revealed the seam a few feet below the surface.

The earliest evidence of coprolite or fossil digging in the Swaffhams was in early 1855. It is likely that work had started over the 1854-55 winter once the harvest was completed. The villagers who farmed Bottisham Poor's Fen had been raising them without paying any royalty to the landowner, Bottisham Parish

Charity. The churchwardens and parish overseers got advice from Clement Francis, a Cambridge solicitor who had recently bought the manorial rights of Stow cum Quy and lived at Quy Hall. Francis advised them to issue a note of trespass in the press. This was duly published in the Cambridge Chronicle in January 1855.

> *"**BOTTISHAM**. Poor's Fen - In consequence of persons digging and carrying away coprolites or clay in this fen, a notice has been issued by the churchwardens of the parish, cautioning all persons that such practices are "unauthorised and illegal." In future any persons offending in either respect will be prosecuted."*
>
> (Cambridge Chronicle, 20th January 1855)

There was a similar situation with so called illegal diggings on common land in Coton, a mile west of Cambridge. There the churchwardens found that the legal fees that had to be expended in ejecting the men proved an obstacle. (O'Connor, B. (1999), 'The Coton Fossil Diggings', Bernard O'Connor, Everton) Whether a formal agreement was subsequently drawn up allowing them to be raised from Poor's Fen has not been evidenced but owners of nearby fen land that contained the fossils would almost certainly have had them extracted. Unfortunately, many of the small landowners' records have not come to light. When several hundred tons were being raised from each acre and coprolite contractors were paying royalties of between six and fifteen shillings a ton (£0.30 - £0.75) it realised considerably more than agricultural rents. They were often less than £1.00 per acre per annum. After the costs of labour, plant and machinery, contractors were able to make considerable profits selling them to the manure manufacturers.

There were workings recorded in nearby Reach in 1855 and at Northills (now called Northfields) Farm in Horningsea the following year. (See author's accounts for Bottisham, Reach and Horningsea; Camb.Chron. 20th Jan.1855) A few years later in the winter of 1857 the Cambridge Chronicle reported

> **"REACH. COPROLITE DIGGERS RECEIVE SURCHARGES.** - We find an impression exists that the coprolites at Reach, (a hamlet in this parish) produce such gain to the persons getting the seam there, that all of them who are digging fossils have this year received surcharges under schedule D of the Income and Property Act and have with others, on the 7th inset., made a journey to "Bottisham Swan" to appeal. We understand that, with the exception of the three persons, there were no other appellants in the district except from this parish."
>
> (Cambridge Chronicle 12th December,1857,p.5)

Only three people seemed a small number given the profits to be made but it does suggest that other coprolite diggers had agreed to the surcharges. These diggings provided employment for many hundreds of men and undoubtedly many local men and boys would have been attracted to the better paid work in the coprolite pits. In May 1857 the Cambridge Chronicle reported the first case of an accident in the local pits. (Cambridge Chronicle 12th May 1857) Although the article was headed Swaffham Prior it is unknown whether the diggings had started here by this time. Maybe the man was working in Swaffham Bulbeck or Reach.

The seam that lay beneath Swaffham Prior, Reach and Burwell intrigued two geologists, Pennings and Jukes-Brown. They commented that they

> "...exhibited different characters from those obtained nearer Cambridge; there was a much greater proportion of lighter coloured phosphates, and the fossils which occurred among these had not been subjected to much rolling, but retained their shells in a more perfect state than usual."
>
> (Pennings and Jukes-Brown, 'Geology of the Neighbourhood of Cambs.,' 1881, p.38)

Those raised from pits in Fen Ditton were of a grey-black nature and may well have given rise to the term "The Ditton

Treacle Mines". Workmen's clothes would have been quite a job to wash after a week in the pits.

The Allix family owned large estates in this area whose land contained coprolites. Although none of their agreements with their tenants or coprolite contractors have come to light, evidence from their contact with Clement Francis shows that they had them worked. In October 1857 Francis noted in his bill book that Henry Bright, the manager of William Colchester's coprolite works in Cambridgeshire, requested permission from Mr Allix to test land in Swaffham Prior that belonged to the late Mr Crisps. He offered £60 an acre for the 9a.1r.21p. field in the Leas (No.42 on the Enclosure Map) *"being the corner piece abutting Black Drove towards the North and White Drove to the West."* (CCRO. Francis & Co. Bill Books 1857 p.138; 1858, pp.77,157) Four days later Francis noted that Mr. Allix had also been approached by a Mr E. Fordham from Swaffham Bulbeck, offering to dig the same nine acres at ten shillings a ton and £50 an acre. There was obviously competition as he shortly increased it to £60 and then £80 an acre. Fordham's correspondence with Francis showed that he

> *"thought the land would produce a ton a rood and stated he was a poor man and one of a number of men who would dig coprolites but that he could pay nothing in advance."*

(CCRO. Francis Bill Books 1857 p.138)

A ton a rood was only four tons an acre - a meagre yield compared to the several hundred tons elsewhere. Maybe he was deliberately underestimating? Mr. Allix had earlier allowed one of his tenants, a Mr. Kent, to take over Mr. Crisps land *"with power to enter and dig coprolites when and as you might think fit."* However, on November 21st Francis convinced him to accept Bright's offer of £60 *"considering it better to deal with a responsible person than have better terms from a person who was not responsible."* Bright was allowed two and a half years to work the field, to erect two washmills and had to compensate

Mr. Kent for the loss of income whilst the fields were out of cultivation. A week later a "*rich vein*" was reported found on land opposite Bright's field. (Ibid.) Maybe it was on one of these workings where the following accident occurred in mid-November that year.

> "*...men digging fossils in the fen conveyed into the village a young man whose horse fell down and rolled on him, breaking his leg.*"
> (Camb.Chron.14th Nov.1857)

Demand for coprolite land increased land values considerably. In January 1858 a plot of almost sixteen acres of fen land in Swaffham Bulbeck, occupied by Richard Blinko, was auctioned. The sale particulars revealed that "*several lots are supposed to contain valuable beds of Coprolites being in close contiguity to other beds now in work.*" (Camb.Chron.30th Jan.1858)

In May 1858 Samuel Chapman, one of the coprolite diggers from Swaffham Prior, appeared in court charged with assault. One Saturday evening, after being in the pub, he threw a local married woman, Margaret Badock through a gap in the hedge into the ditch and "*grossly abused her.*" At the Petty Sessions he pleaded ignorance of the matter through being drunk and was subsequently sentenced to four years imprisonment with hard labour. Reflecting concern at the potential impact on local village life the judge gave a warning to the men that, "*they cannot commit such outrages with impunity and claim drunkenness as an excuse.*" (Cambridge Chronicle 1st May 1858 p5.)

A fortnight later further evidence in the local press shows that another member of the parish gentry was involved. The Cambridge Chronicle reported that"*...men raising coprolites in fen land belonging to Revd. T. Preston, discovered some four or five feet in the clay, the skeletons of two humans.*" (Camb.Chron.15th May 1858) Further details about the find have not emerged. It is quite likely that all the local landowners and farmers with property on the Greensand arranged to have the coprolites raised. However, few of their records have come to light. There were also speculators involved. They bought coprolite land, sold the rights to raising the bed to a coprolite contractor and then sold the field for a higher price once it had been restored.

With the work on the "other beds" the diggings provided valuable employment opportunities. Evidence shows that outside labour had migrated to these diggings, notably from the coprolite parishes in Suffolk and gangs that came over from Ireland. This introduced a new experience for the Swaffhams. There had been additional farm labourers during the busy seasons but nothing on this scale. It must have seemed that an army had encamped in the area - but potentially for years!. As a result this influx of males increased the social problems in the area with overcrowding of the small, cramped cottages, drunkenness, brawling, theft and rape. Some entrepreneurs profited from the diggings by opening beerhouses, providing cheaply built hovels and in some cases opening shops or providing other services. Hoards of men were catered for in the public houses but numerous beerhouses opened across the coprolite belt. Local villagers made extra cash by providing lodgings. There were reports of men staying in tents by the roadside with their families, of men sleeping in the pubs, in barns or in horse-drawn barracks that were brought in specifically for the purpose. In May 1858 hundreds of them attended Reach Fair on Fair Green.

> *"600 Diggers In The Neighbourhood - Reach Fair. The public houses got well patronized; and what is more, good order seemed to prevail amongst the coprolite diggers numbering nearly 600 in the neighbourhood, and we hear of no disturbances taking place of any consequence. This may be considered due, partly, to the good and excellent precaution and management of Inspector Dade, of this division who had several officers on the spot in readiness if required."*

(Cambridge Chronicle, 15th May 1858, p.5)

The *"good order"* was probably due to the court case a fortnight earlier. The proximity of the diggings increased property values of some premises. In late June 1858, the Cambridge Chronicle advertised a sale to those involved in the coprolite business.

> "*Mercantile premises at Commercial End. Wharf and navigation. Good district for trade in Agriculture, Manures, and are within a mile of extensive Coprolite Beds.*"
> (Camb.Chron.26th June 1858)

Whilst it may have been the same property the following month there was an auction of a corn mill, granary, coal shed, private lode and wharfage in Swaffham Prior. The sale particulars included a similar description in that the premises were "*well situated for trade in AGRICULTURAL MANURES and are within a mile of extensive COPROLITE beds.*" (CUL. PSQ.18.153)

Neighbouring farmers and landowners must have been aware of the profits being made by Mr Allix, Revd. Preston and others raising coprolites. Average prices for Cambridgeshire coprolites rose from forty-three shillings and six pence (£2.18) a ton in 1856 to forty-eight shillings (£2.40) in 1858. In autumn 1859 Nathaniel Johnson, the agent for Edward Packard, another Ipswich manure manufacturer, asked for Allix's permission to "sound" some of his fields that were tenanted by John Kent. He offered £50 an acre. Kent, as mentioned earlier, was already raising them from other fields belonging to Allix. The request was refused but no explanation was given. Maybe they were set aside for Kent when his labourers had finished his workings. Not long afterwards Allix purchased some fields in Swaffham Prior from Mr. and Mrs. Benjamin Kent and then allowed "*John Day and others*" to raise the coprolites from them. Surprisingly, the royalty was only five shillings (£0.25) a ton. Was this an early example of philanthropy or was it a bit of nepotism? Whether they were relatives, local farmers or friends is unknown but it is likely that they would have employed local men rather than outsiders. Mr. Johnson was subsequently allowed some of Allix's land in Reach when he increased his offer to £60 an acre. (CCRO. Francis & Co. bill books, Sept. 1858, p.395; 21st November 1859)

That same year, 1859, evidence shows that another local clergyman was involved. Rev. Frederick Maberley had men raising them from thirty acres of Sedge Fen and Turf Fen, about four miles to the northeast of Swaffham Prior by Reach Lode. This was in forfeit of a £3,000 mortgage he had on the property with the Dean and Chapter of Ely Cathedral. Their treasurer and agent considered that he was "*incapable of managing his affairs*" and suspended the forfeiture in January 1860 and made him pay £30, the estimated value of the coprolites. (CCRO.283B12/64) This was surprisingly little in the circumstances but it is undocumented as to whether they subsequently arranged a lease with another contractor.

In July 1859, when Stephen Danby's estate in Bottisham and Swaffham Prior was auctioned at the Red Lion, the sale particulars described it as

> "*Several Allotments and Inclosures of Remarkably Productive Accommodation Land with valuable beds of COPROLITE & CLUNCH Comprising an Area of about 50 Acres of Arable and Grass land.*"
>
> (CCRO. R51/25/31(G))

There was no indication who the purchaser was but, given the surge in interest in the mineral, there is every likelihood that the fossils would have been worked. Perhaps it was on one of these workings that the following accident occurred.

> "**SWAFFHAM PRIOR.** *Accident.- A person named Whitehead, who has wife and six children dependent on his labour, was working in the Fen with several others raising coprolites, and when picking out or excavating the earth some few feet from and under the surface, a quantity of soil or earth fell onto his leg thereby breaking the same, which was heard to crack by the other men in the same cutting. He was immediately conveyed to hospital.*"
>
> (Cambridge Chronicle 10th March 1860 p5.)

The beds also extended onto land belonging to the Revd. Hailstone, who lived at Anglesey Abbey. He called upon Francis' services whose notebooks revealed that on September 15th 1860 James Headly, the Cambridge iron founder, won an agreement to dig ten acres of Rev. Hailstone's estate that was being farmed by John Ellis. (CCRO. Francis Bill Books A-N 1860 p.294) Headly won numerous agreements in parishes across the coprolite belt and supplied the workings with plant and machinery made in his coprolite factory behind his foundry on Mill Road, Cambridge. Francis' bill books also show that six weeks later on November 21st Messrs. Allix gave John Masters, a merchant from King's Lynn, a licence to work them in Swaffham Bulbeck. A month later Colonel Allix gave Mr Preston a licence to work a field in the same parish. Exact details of these agreements have not come to light but when Mr. Masters fell behind in his payments Francis ensured that he promptly sent the sum of £157 10s.1d.

With so many workings in the area it was surprising that the 1861 census showed Swaffham Bulbeck's population fell by fifteen over the decade to 873. None of the men in the parish actually described themselves as "diggers". Yet 69-year old John Ellis who was living on Village Street was described as *"Farmer of 650 acres, 20 men, 10 boys Farm work, 10 digging coperalites [sic]"*. The misspelling gives one an idea of the local accent. Could he have been providing the labour for Headly or were these his own workings? It is therefore likely that that the work was dominated by local farmers who engaged their agricultural labourers in the work during the off-season.

Swaffham Prior's population saw a similar fall of fifty-five to 1329. There was only one described as a *"fossil digger"* but 35-year old David Picken described himself as a *"Coprolite Worker employing 35 men and 7 boys."* That makes a total of fifty-three in both parishes. Despite this there were many simply described as *"labourers"* who were probably engaged in the workings. Of the 116 described as involved in the fenland parishes forty-three lived in Reach, thirty-two in Burwell, fifteen in Cambridge, four in Chesterton, two in Horningsea and two in Fen Ditton. What had happened to the 600 diggers of three years earlier? (CCRO.1861 census)

No further evidence of what happened in 1861 - 2 have emerged except that in November 1862 Francis notified Mr. Johnson of the poor state of the ditches with a demand that his workmen put them in proper order. (CCRO. Francis Bill Books A-N 1862 p.229) At the beginning of February 1863, Downing College, Cambridge got involved. They signed a lease with John Ellis, the tenant of their farm in Swaffham Bulbeck, to work the fossils on Heath Farm. The college documents indicated that it was in Swaffham Prior but its exact location has not been determined. He agreed to pay them a royalty of £60 per acre. Although no surveyor maps that might show the extent of the diggings have emerged, their correspondence shows that twenty-three acres were worked before his death in 1867. His executor, Richard Ellis, then took over the lease and continued the operation into the 1870s. (Downing College Mun. Swaffham Prior)

In March 1863, Francis drew up a further agreement for Mr. Allix allowing Mr. Masters five acres from the 6a.3r.19. field in Sedge Fen on the Dean and Chapter of Ely's land. He agreed on the same £70 an acre. (Ibid.1863 pp.167, 181, 469-70)

In 1864, in the vicar of Swaffham Prior's report to the Ecclesiastical Commissioners on the state of the parish, he described it as of 5,297 acres with a population of 1329.

"The district is agricultural but the digging and washing of coprolites which are found in some portions of the parish furnish employment to many."

(CCRO. Church Commission Files, 1980 Swaffham Prior, 25/11/1864)

Evidence suggests that they may also have been raised on the 373a.0r.12p. Church Farm in Swaffham Bulbeck, tenanted by

George Hemmington Harris. In the 1864 report the Church Commissioners pointed out that *"The district is purely agricultural although some additional labour has been required in getting coprolites."* Whilst they could have been engaged by Mr. Harris no records of any agreements have come to light.

Whether the work was continuous through the late-1860s is uncertain. Following John Ellis' death the trustees and Mrs Ellis auctioned 150 acres of land in Bottisham Fen. The sale particulars described five lots totalling 57a.3r.32p. which were *"believed to contain rich beds of coprolites."* They were situated alongside and west of Swaffham Lode, north of the parish pits and east of Forty Acre Drove. Mr Swan, possibly the Cambridge coprolite merchant and beer seller, bought the Hare and Hounds with its adjacent ten acres for £1,000. Messrs. Fordham, Aves and York purchased the other plots at £50 an acre, considerably more than those plots without coprolites. One can presume that they then had the coprolites raised. (CUL. PSQ.18.210; Cambridge Folk Museum, SP635/74; O'Connor, B. (1999), 'The Swaffhams' Fossil Diggings,' Bernard O'Connor, Everton) A subsequent article in a geological book suggests that Mr. Packard was involved. Maybe he made purchases from the contractors? (Whitaker, W. (1921), 'Water Supply of Cambs.' Memoirs of the Geological Survey, London, p.55)

In the vicar of Swaffham Prior's 1870 report on the parish to the Church Commissioners he indicated that the industry was still in operation.

> *"Coprolites are found in some parts of this parish but are stated to have been dug on the only portion of the Chapter Estate where they were found to exist... Coprolites exist and have been dug out of some of the leasehold near the Catchwater drain by arrangement. P.F. Palmby holds farm buildings. Mr Allix is a considerable owner in the parish."*

(CCRO. Church Comm. Ely Chapter Estates)

In the autumn of 1870 the Cambridge Chronicle reported another accident in the local pits. Over the years that the diggings were in operation there were numerous cases of accidental deaths by falls, collapses as well as broken limbs and hernias.

> "**ACCIDENT** - An accident occurred in the coprolite pits in Swaffham Bulbeck fen, on Tuesday last, to a young man by the name of William Crane, of Bottisham. The poor fellow was employed in filling with earth where fossils had been taken out; the earth slipped and fell on him. Though watchers were employed they did not perceive the danger, when all at once the earth fell in, and completely smothered him. His fellow labourers set to work and extricated him. He was conveyed to the hospital at Cambridge. Although much hurt we hope he is progressing favourably."
>
> (Cambridge Chronicle 22nd October 1870 p.4.)

Following the death of Mrs Sarah Allix her and C. P. Allix's 248 acre estate in Swaffham Prior, Swaffham Bulbeck and Reach was auctioned in November 1870 but the sale particulars made no mention of coprolites. (CUL. PSQ.18.218) The shallower deposits were worked first and these may well have been exhausted. There were still workings in other parts of the fen. Their value was referred to in an 1871 report to the Government regarding the income of the University Colleges. Downing College's response admitted receiving an average coprolite revenue of £337 per annum. When an agricultural worker might only make £25 a year in wages this sum could have bought a small estate. The report explained why all the deposit had not been exhausted, "...There are but a few more acres to be dug and the stone lies very deep." (CUL. Report on University Income, Downing College)

In some parishes the "diggers" were considered an unruly, drunken and irreligious lot but, although nothing has emerged about the social life of the diggers in the Swaffhams, parish records show that in 1870 at least some of them had their children baptised in church. (CCRO. 253/2/B1)

The 1871 census showed Swaffham Bulbeck's population experienced a 6% increase of fifty-seven over the decade to 912. Fifty-three men and boys were described as directly involved in the industry. They were generally young men in their twenties with an average age of 22.5. The eldest was sixty-eight and the youngest fourteen. As 81.1% were locally born, and 16.9% were from other Cambridgeshire villages, it was very much dominated by locals. Swaffham Prior's population had a 3% increase of forty people to 1369. 35-year old Mark Scott was *"Foreman of Coprolite Works"* and .one man, 49-year old William Todd, described himself as an *"invalid coprolite labourer."* A further thirty-eight were described as employed in the diggings. Their average age was 26.8 with the eldest 58 and the youngest 11. Only 17.9% were recorded as born in the parish, with 74.3% from other Cambridgeshire villages, mostly from Reach. This confirms there had been a significant inward migration of labour.

The table below shows a comparison of the age structure of the 1871 workforce from the two villages and one can see some significant differences.

Age Group of diggers	Swaffham Bulbeck	Swaffham Prior
11-14	2	3
15-19	8	13
20-25	16	5
26-30	10	6
over 30	15	12
Total	51	39

(CCRO. 1871 census)

Of the 863 recorded in the census as involved in the fenland diggings one hundred and sixty-nine were in Wicken, the highest number in the whole of the coprolite belt. There were one hundred in Cambridge, ninety-five in Horningsea, eighty-four in Burwell, fifty-five in Fen Ditton, forty-six in Bottisham, thirty-two in Chesterton and seven in Upware. And that was only the number of people described by the enumerator as involved. How many other labourers and agricultural labourers were employed is unknown.

If, as seems the case, it was farmers who were more involved than outside contractors, then employing teenagers would have been cheaper than older men. Richard Ellis, presumably was their major employer and records show that his labourers had worked thirty-three acres before the diggings came to a close in 1876. This meant that, at least on this one farm, over fifty acres were worked. Receiving royalties of over £3,000 would have been a very welcome addition to Downing College's coffers since farm rentals were rarely over thirty shillings (£1.50) per acre at this time. Mr. Ellis would have profited too. Selling on average 250 tons per acre to manure manufacturers at up to £3 per ton the income would have realised at least £30,000 before costs! (Downing College, Mun. Swaffham)

How long the work provided an extra income for local men is unknown but no further evidence of diggings in Swaffham Bulbeck has emerged. The only indirect evidence was when a survey of Chalk Farm, a mile and a half to the southeast of the village, revealed that it had "*a building for mixing artificial manures.*" This suggests that, to avoid paying for expensive fertiliser from the manufacturers, some farmers were mixing it on site. (see author's account of Whaddon; CCRO. Church Comm. Files, Ely Chapter Estates, Swaffham Bulbeck)

The ending of the Franco-Prussian War in 1870 led to a period of peace and prosperity across Europe. Farmers wanted to increase food production and this generated even more demand for fertilisers. As a result manure manufacturers increased their demand for coprolites and average prices for the Cambridgeshire ones rose to sixty-five shillings (£3.25) a ton in 1872. This made working the deeper seams a profitable venture. This may explain why, when the Manor of Burgh Hall became vacant in 1873, the sale particulars pointed out that "*there are valuable BEDS OF COPROLITES in this parish which may eventually affect the value of the rights of the Lord of the Manor.*" The 230a.0r.34p. estate sold for £16,100 with John Kent buying the manorial rights for £700. He must have profited greatly from his coprolite interests over the years. However, on his death, sixteen years later, the estate was sold for only £8,000. (CUL. PSQ.18.241) What happened that caused such a decline?

In May 1877 the 194a.2r.34p. Lordship Farm was auctioned and described as "*fine arable, pasture and fen land*". The sale particulars pointed out that

> "*There are Valuable Beds of Coprolites upon the Freehold of the Estate, which may be raised to great advantage, the water carriage contiguous to the estate offering great facilities for the disposal of them to the Trade.*"
> (CUL. PSQ.18.300)

It was sold to a Mr Mainprice for £12,000 but it is undocumented as to whether he arranged their extraction.. The following year the sale particulars for an auction of "The Slates" revealed that Robert Mason of Reach had been working it. When it went up for sale in August 1878 it was pointed out that

> "*about 4 acres of the land, which had been dug for Coprolites, now remains unlevelled, but the Tenant is bound by Agreement to level the same in a proper and customary manner fit for Agricultural use.*"
> (CUL. PSQ.18.311)

Why did Mason leave the land unlevelled? One reason was that the last four years of the 1870s were dominated by heavy rain. This had a dramatic effect on the coprolite diggings. Increased rainfall made the work in the pits dangerous. In Ashwell Museum one can see the "creepers", iron grips fastened over the sole of the boot to stop slipping in wet mud. It also increased pumping costs with the additional water and made it difficult to properly dry out the slurry. The increased costs made the business less economic for the coprolite contractors. Spending money on levelling pits was not considered worthwhile but some contractors were compelled to under the agreement they signed in their contract with the landowner. The wet weather might also explain why Richard Ellis finished his workings in 1876.

The heavy rain also affected farmers. The waterlogged soil spoilt many of the seedlings and summer storms destroyed many crops. Harvests were dramatically reduced. Farmers profits fell and with food production much lowered the then Tory government's introduced Free Trade. This allowed entrepreneurs to capitalise on the newly developed refrigerated shipping and import vast quantities of cheap meat and grain surpluses from the American Prairies and South American Pampas into Great Britain. Home prices plummeted. Wheat prices fell to a half of what they were in the 1860s. Many farmers went out of business. Some tried to arrange rent reductions and managed to get up to 30% but others were evicted. Many farms were untenanted and there was a knock on effect on other local businesses. Huge numbers of agricultural and other labourers were forced to accept lower wages or were laid off.

On top of this, newly discovered rock phosphate from Charleston, South Carolina, had started to be shipped into British ports in the early-1870s. In 1876 coprolite production was 258,150 tons. The following year it dropped to 69,006 tons whilst 170,000 tons of American phosphate was imported with a value of £500,000. These rock phosphates were very similar in nature to the East Anglian coprolites but, in true American fashion, they were on a far greater scale and variety. The Charleston News and Courier of 1880 reported that

"These deposits consist of nodules of phosphate of lime, thickly interspersed with the huge bones and teeth of antediluvian mammalian and marine mammoths of stupendous and gigantic proportions; the chrysonicocrisides, ichthyosauri, hadrosauri, stupendous giant baboons, prodigious mammoth gorillas, lizards 33 feet long, and other huge graminovorous and carnivorous quadrupeds; also the squaladons, phocodons, dinotherinons, and members of the ichthaurian, saurian and cetacean families, whales 500 feet long, sharks 200 feet long, briny leviathons, voracious marine vultures and other monster, rapacious denizens of the mighty deep - land and water animals lying in the same bed. These wonderful and awe-inspiring skeleton remains, styled by Professor Agassiz "the greatest cemetery in the world," constitute by far the most valuable fertiliser known to man since the exhaustion of the Peruvian guano deposits; and are an inexhaustible source of wealth to the State and people of South Carolina, and thence to the whole world."

(Charleston News and Courier, Industrial Issue, (1880))

It was a thick seam of shallow depth around the estuary mouth and the companies working it employed cheap Black labour to dig it out. It had a higher quality phosphate content than the British coprolite and even with transport costs it sold in Great Britain at much cheaper rates. Domestic prices dropped an average of 20% to £2.40 a ton. This made many operations uneconomic. In many parishes pits were abandoned, coprolite contractors asked to be allowed reductions of their leases. Some landowners agreed but others refused and forced them to continue with the terms of their agreement and forcing them into bankruptcy. Coprolite labourers joined the many other unemployed in the area. Production fell to 30,500 tons in 1880. The Agricultural Depression had set in.

Manure manufacturers suffered too. Farmers were not buying fertilisers to grow food they could not sell. The prices of "super" fell to as low as five pounds ten shillings (£5.50) a ton. This downward spiral in trade came full circle when the manure manufacturers stopped purchases of the overseas phosphates. There was no market for "super". The decline in the industry's fortune was varied. Aware of the industry's changing fortune, some of the early coprolite entrepreneurs sold up. Many contractors, like Mr. Packard, pulled out of uneconomic ventures and concentrated in parishes where there were still seams worth exploiting. As in farming, wages were reduced which meant many of the younger men looked for work elsewhere.

In this area there were still pits in operation in Horningsea which attracted diggers from the Swaffhams. To get to work they had to walk over the fields which annoyed some of the local farmers. They complained to the Trustees of Bottisham Charities and the minutes of their meeting revealed that the problem was caused by,

> "...continued trespass of land of large numbers of coprolite diggers going to and from Horningsea. Paths had been made in several directions. In particular over No.48 and injury done to the ditches, and the men had them used threatening and abusive language expressing a resolve to go where they pleased across the fen."

> (Extract from minutes Bottisham United Charities 28th July 1879)

Farmers reduced demand for "super" caused almost identical problems for the American suppliers as those experienced by the British coprolite contractors. The South Carolina Ministry of Agriculture described the problem in early 1880 as being

> "...a very general and widespread depression prevailing in the production of river rock. As is generally known, the great bulk of this rock is shipped to foreign countries. The short crops, and general agricultural distress which has for some years past spread over the whole of Europe, had most seriously affected the capacity of the farmer to purchase and pay for fertilisers, and consequently diminished to a very

large degree the demand for the Carolina rock. Thus not only was the market lost, to a great extent, but the prices at which the rock could be sold were very greatly diminished. In consequence of this, river mining became unprofitable. A large number of the smaller companies ceased work entirely, and even the larger ones were compelled very greatly to curtail their operations and to continue with a much reduced force and at great loss."

('First Annual Report of the Commissioner of Agriculture of the State of South Carolina.' Walker, Evans & Cogswell, Charleston, (1880), pp.11-12.)

Some of the smaller manure manufacturers helped revive the coprolite trade. With American supplies much reduced in 1880 many renewed their demand for coprolite, albeit at lower prices. Inland manufacturers, like Colchester and Ball of Burwell, Birds of Duxford, the Fordhams of Odsey and the Farmers Manure Company of Royston had many directors and shareholders on their boards who still had coprolite land. The Chairman of the latter company, Joseph Nunn, had an extensive deposit on his Bassingbourn Farm. The cost of freighting in the new phosphates was high and there was a policy of wanting to ensure a continuing business for some of their customers who might otherwise have been in financial difficulties. As a result some parishes managed to maintain their coprolite industry during this difficult period but the diggings in the Swaffhams seemingly came to an end.

The 1881 census showed a dramatic reduction in the population of both parishes. Numbers in Swaffham Bulbeck fell 18%, a decline of 168 people to 744. Swaffham Prior's population fell 20% to 1078. This was 281 lower and the biggest fluctuation that century. There was no mention of anyone as involved in the industry at all. Closer comparison of the 1871 and 1881 census may show what occupations the diggers then took on and how many left the area.

Of the 101 described in the 1881 census as employed in the industry in the fenland parishes there were thirty in Burwell, eleven in Cambridge, nine in Bottisham, nine in Wicken, six in Fen Ditton, four in Horningsea and one in Stow-cum-Quy.

The coming of the railway to the east side of the river in 1884 revived the coprolite trade in those parishes that still had accessible seams. Clement Francis paid to have some sidings constructed beside the line at Quy. This may well have contributed to the opening of a cement works in Swaffham Prior where some of the unemployed diggers probably found work. However, by summer 1887, further evidence of the demise of the coprolite industry came when the Hare and Hounds was put up for sale. The lack of trade when the diggings ceased must have contributed to its closure. Interestingly, there was still a bed of coprolites in the adjoining field which was being worked for the chalk marl.

> *"At Swaffham Prior,*
> *A Brick and Slate House (Late the Hare and Hounds) and Freehold Land adjoining containing 10a.1r.28p. From the top strata of which a natural Portland Cement is being made, and a part also contains a VALUABLE BED OF COPROLITES"*

(Cambridge Independent Press 18th June 1887)

Maybe this bed was raised as the following year, following Francis' death, the industry's fortunes revived. The reason was entirely philanthropic. The social problems caused by the Agricultural Depression had left many families without a regular source of income. Numbers on parish relief increased which caused increased costs for those businesses still in operation. To alleviate some of the problems Lady Francis, the Lady of Quy and Fen Ditton Manor, allowed the many unemployed diggers in the area to raise the coprolites from the fen without them having to pay a royalty. There had been considerable tension in the late-

1860s regarding Quy Fen when Mr. Francis had an injunction slapped on the commoners who were raising coprolites on what they considered Common Land on the fen without paying any royalties. (See author's accounts of Stow cum Quy, Fen Ditton and Horningsea)

Maybe the tenant of King's College, Manor Farm in Horningsea shared Mrs Francis' ideals as in spring 1889 the Cambridge Chronicle reported on an improvement in the situation.

HORNINGSEA. FOSSIL WORKS RE-OPENED. - *A boon to the unemployed. Mr. Banyard opened his coprolite workings at Horningsea giving work to 70 men and boys."*

(Cambridge Chronicle, 1st February 1889)

This philanthropy may also have been manifested in this parish as the 1890 6-inch map, seen in the illustrations, shows two "Coprolite Works" in Swaffham Prior. The 25 inch maps, shown in the illustrations. detail the sites but it is unknown who was responsible for them. Two washmills, a pump, an engine and other sheds can be seen with a tramway allowing horses or steam engines to haul truckloads of the fossils down Forty Acre Droveway to be transhipped onto the Great Eastern Railway. (6-inch Cambs. XLI.NW (1890); 25" Cambs.XLI.2, XLI.6; GR.548642 and 540643) Following the death of John Kent his estate was sold in 1889 for £8,000, half the price he paid for it in 1873. (CUL. PSQ.18.241) The fall in land values with the exhaustion of the coprolite deposit meant some speculators made heavy losses.

As in 1881 there was no evidence of anyone as involved in the industry in the 1891 census. Swaffham Bulbeck's population had increased over the decade by fifty-six to 800. Swaffham Prior's population decreased by seventy-two to 1006. There had been an increase in the numbers employed in other parishes however. Of the 117 described as involved in the 1891 census there were fifty-three in Bottisham, thirty-two in Fen Ditton, twenty-two in Burwell, one in Cambridge and one in Wicken. (CCRO. 1891 census)

Although the revival stimulated work in other parishes, notably on Quy Fen and Horningsea, the coal dock strike and coal strike of 1890 increased costs. Labour costs and freight rates rose and by 1894 other countries were exporting their own superphosphate to Britain. The Quy Fen Coprolite Works went bankrupt and the plant and machinery were auctioned in 1894. Many men and their families lost a regular income and, although what effect this had on the village economy has not been documented, it is likely that many entered the workhouse or left the area to find alternative employment. Local craftsmen and traders would have lost business with the loss of income when the works closed.

Although during the First World War there was a brief revival of the diggings at Horningsea, it appeared the remaining coprolites lie forgotten out under the Fen. Evidence today of the workings is still quite noticeable. Aerial photographs of the fen edge show a ribbed pattern in the fields indicating the progression of the trenches. Long white stripes show clay that was brought to the surface during digging and not replaced with topsoil. As there was no money available to pay any labourers to fill in and level the cuts, many long narrow lakes, some filled with reed beds with overgrown banks of unreplaced subsoil can be seen on Stow cum Quy Fen north of Allicky Farm and south-west of Bottisham Lode. In fact, they have proved a valuable addition to the fen as they now provide natural habitat for many birds and insects in a countryside otherwise scarce of foliage. (Grove, R. (1976), 'The Cambridgeshire Coprolite Mining Rush', pp.39-41; Worsam and Taylor, 'Geology of County of Cambs.'1969, p121)

www.ingramcontent.com/pod-product-compliance
Lightning Source LLC
Chambersburg PA
CBHW071411040426
42444CB00009B/2198